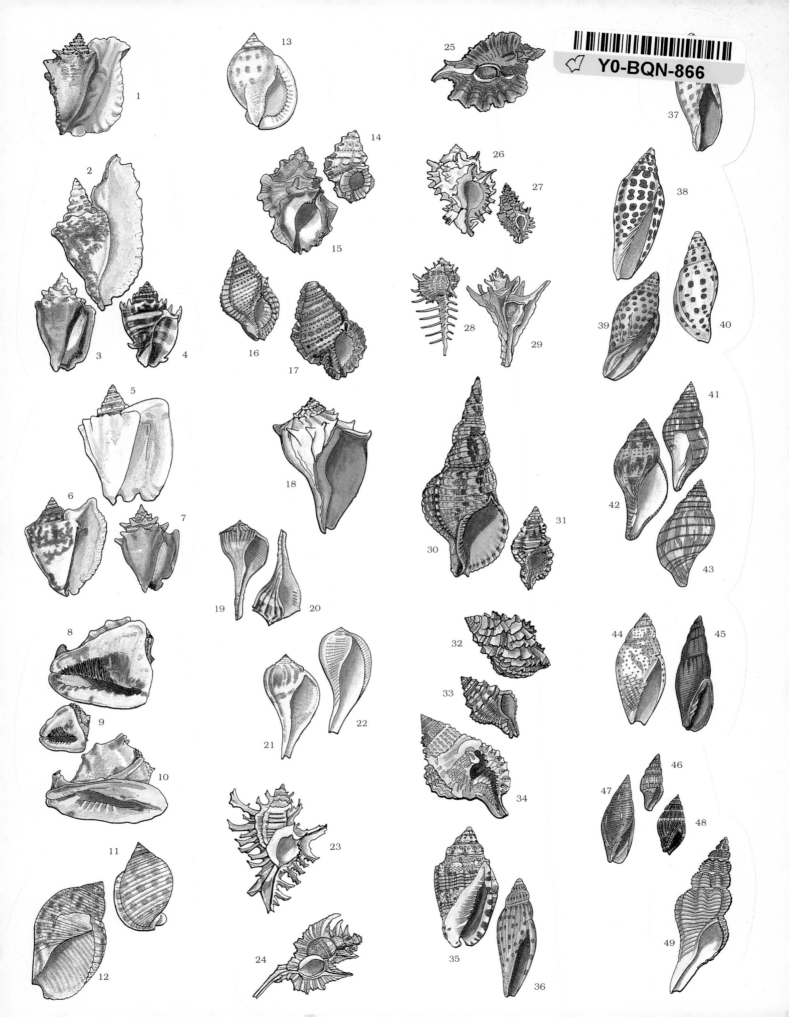

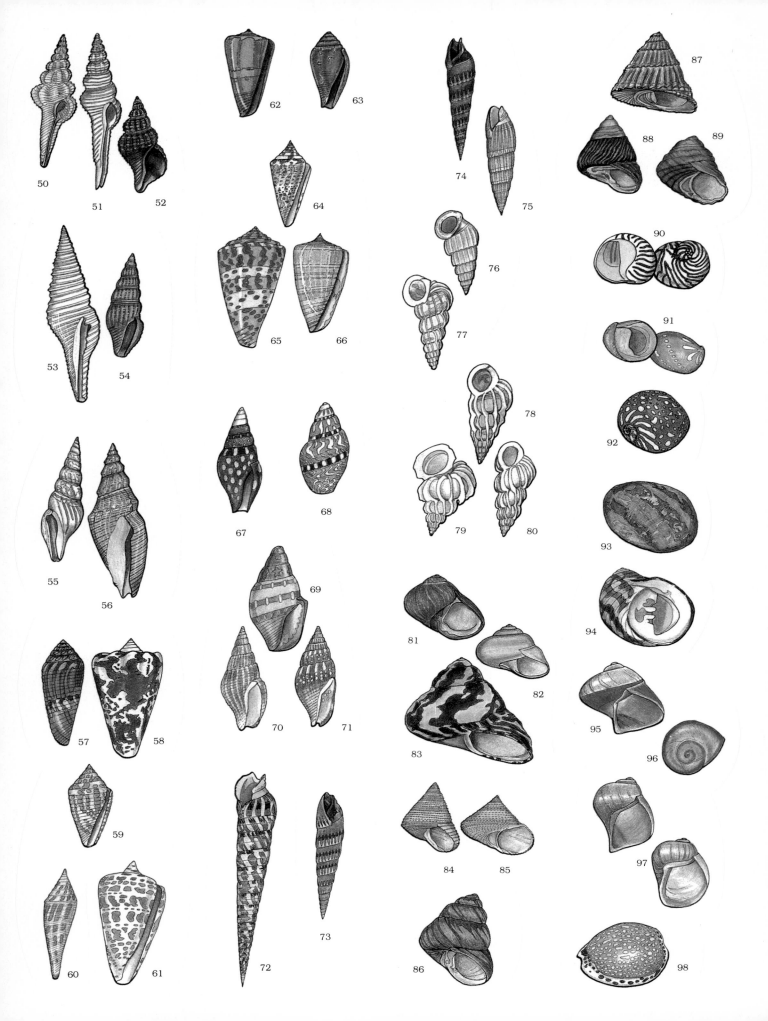

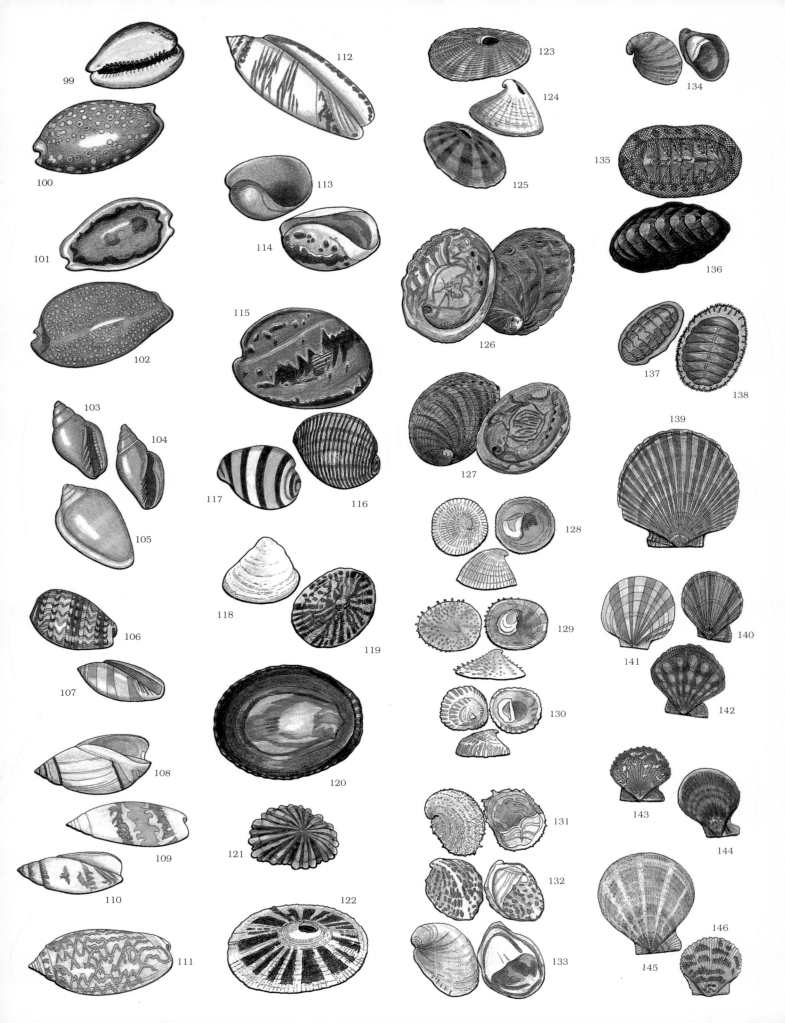

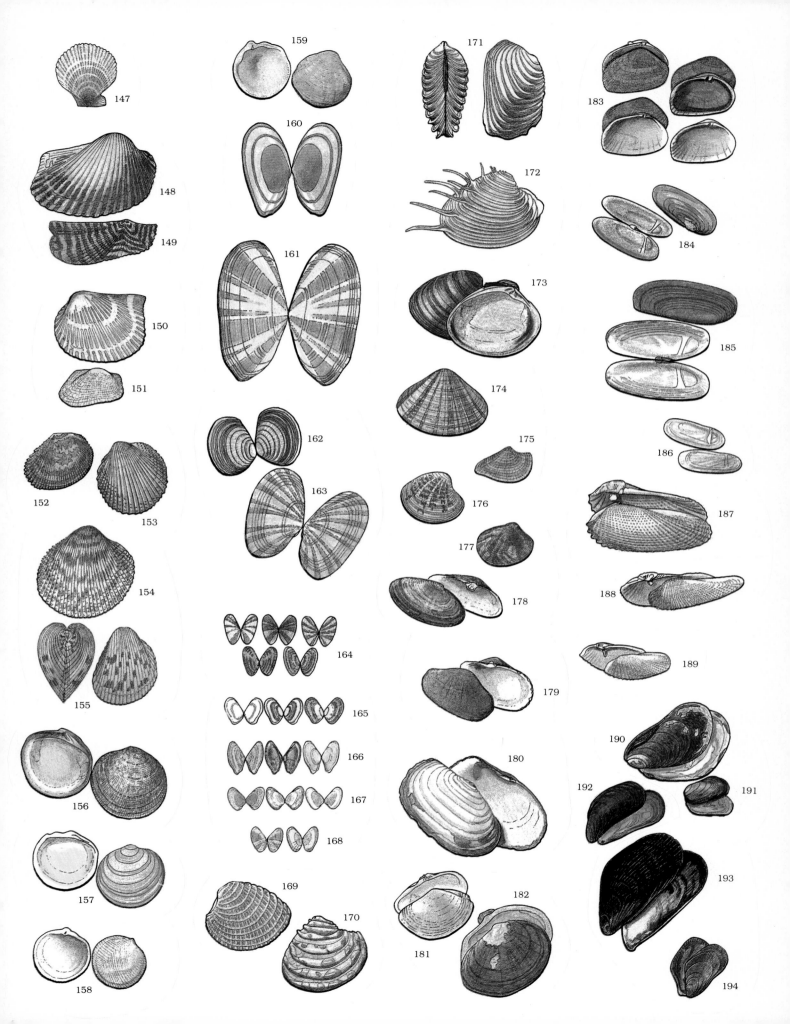

Peterson Field Guide Color-In Books

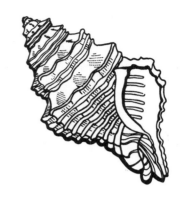

Shells

Jackie Leatherbury Douglass and John Douglass

*Roger Tory Peterson and
Dr. Harald A. Rehder, Consulting Editors*

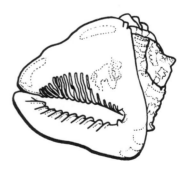

*Sponsored by the
National Wildlife Federation
and the Roger Tory Peterson Institute*

Houghton Mifflin Company Boston New York

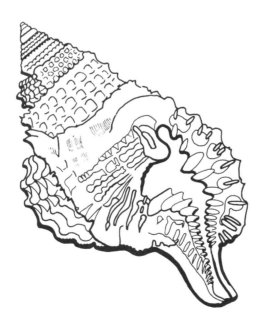

Copyright © 1985 by
Houghton Mifflin Company

All rights reserved.

For information about permission to
reproduce selections from this book,
write to Permissions,
Houghton Mifflin Company,
215 Park Avenue South,
New York, New York 10003.

Visit our Web site:
www.houghtonmifflinbooks.com.

ISBN-10: 0-618-54223-X
ISBN-13: 978-0-618-54223-9

Printed in the United States of America

DPI 10 9 8 7 6 5 4 3 2 1

Introduction

Finding shells, or "shelling," is a visual activity, a hobby that trains the eye. Most of us, if we are at all interested, soon acquire a copy of *A Field Guide to Shells of the Atlantic and Gulf Coasts* or its western counterpart, *A Field Guide to Pacific Coast Shells.* The beautiful photographs in these handy, pocket-sized books are arranged so that one kind of shell can readily be separated from another.

When I was a boy, in the early decades of this century, many lads my age collected bird's eggs; they were a popular outlet for that craving of all children to collect things. Today, taking bird's eggs is forbidden. Although butterflies are easily collectible and so are minerals (more so than plants), none of nature's varied productions lend themselves more to the gratification of the collecting instinct than shells. Because of their texture and delicate coloring, shells have some of the same tactile and visual appeal of jewels, jade, and fine porcelain; and inasmuch as the shell found on the beach is but the lifeless garment of the once-living mollusk, there is no harm in collecting it.

This coloring book will sharpen your observations and condition your memory for the days you spend at the beach. By filling in the colors during evenings at home or on winter days while dreaming of summer at the shore, you will be better informed about these same shells should you chance to find them.

A coloring book such as this will help your color perception, but it will not teach you how to draw, unless you copy the basic line drawings so artfully prepared by John Douglass. You might even try to sketch from your own specimens, if only roughly in pencil.

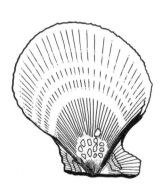

Exploring the beach, watching the shorebirds and other inhabitants of the tideline, and searching for shells can be many things — an art, a science, a game, or a sport — but above all, it is an absorbing activity that sharpens the senses, especially the eye and the sense of touch. When you pick up a shell, trace its contours with your fingers. If you draw or paint, this will also bring the sense of touch into play: the images of the eye and the mind are transferred by hand to paper. In the process you become more aware of the natural world — the real world — and inevitably you become an environmentalist.

Most of you will find colored pencils best suited for coloring this book, but if you are handy with brushes and paints, you may prefer to fill in the outlines with watercolors. Crayons, too, can be used. But don't labor; have fun. This is what exploring the beach, finding shells, and this coloring book are all about.

Roger Tory Peterson

About This Book

When I was a small child, I used to sit for hours holding and examining the Queen Conch my father and mother brought back home to me from their trip to Florida. I put the shell to my ear to hear the sounds of the sea. Immediately, I was transported to times and places unknown. I could even smell the lingering scent of the salty sea air. As I sat and dreamed with that shell in my hands, I remember thinking that those splendid pink colors in its mouth were the most beautiful colors I had ever seen.

I was hooked; from then on I had to have more. I became interested in the shells' simplistic, pure, fine-line shapes. I couldn't believe the difference in the shells — the sizes, and the variety of elegant patterns. Each one is a natural sculpture, a piece of fine art. Most of all I love the colors, whether bright or subdued; they are especially luscious when shells are wet. You can even find beauty in old chipped and faded shells. They are indeed objects to possess and collect.

A good way to learn to recognize different shells is by coloring their shapes. Use colored pencils, crayons, water colors, or markers — any way you like to color best. Sometimes, especially when the shell is white, you might like to just color the background around the shell. Don't worry about getting each one "right" — you must remember that even two shells of the same kind and color may not be exactly the same.

Have fun coloring the drawings in this book. While you're doing it, try to memorize the names that go with the shapes. It is really fun to recognize a shell from a picture you have colored. You'll never forget it. Finding a shell and realizing you know which one it is is just as enjoyable as unwrapping a present that's just for you. Learning to know what things are is giving yourself the best gift of all.

Mollusks

Although most shells we see on a beach are empty, worn fragments that have been battered by the waves, each one once housed an animal called a mollusk. The animals in this group are soft-bodied creatures that may or may not have an exterior shell. The name mollusk is derived from the Latin word *mollis,* meaning "soft bodies, no bones."

As we have a skeleton for support on the inside of our body, most mollusks have a shell on the outside of their body. The shell not only provides support but also helps protect these animals from predators — other animals on land or in water that would use them for food.

All mollusks have an organ known as the mantle. Glands in the mantle use minerals in the water to make a sticky

Five Kinds of Living Mollusks

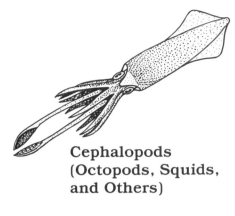

Cephalopods
(Octopods, Squids, and Others)

Pelecypods
(Bivalves)

Gastropods
(Univalves and Others)

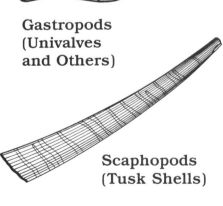

Scaphopods
(Tusk Shells)

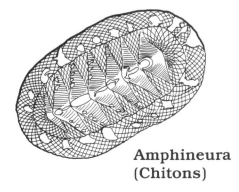

Amphineura
(Chitons)

Gastropod or Sea Snail

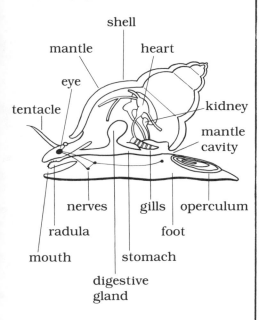

shell
mantle
heart
eye
tentacle
kidney
mantle cavity
nerves
gills
operculum
radula
foot
mouth
stomach
digestive gland

Pelecypod (Bivalve)

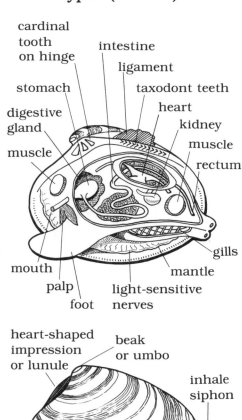

cardinal tooth on hinge
intestine
ligament
stomach
taxodont teeth
digestive gland
heart
kidney
muscle
muscle
rectum
gills
mouth
mantle
palp
light-sensitive nerves
foot

heart-shaped impression or lunule
beak or umbo
inhale siphon
foot
age or growth rings
exhale siphon

fluid that the animal secretes. This sticky fluid hardens into the limy material that makes up the shell.

Gastropods (Univalves and Others). The word gastropod means "stomach-footed." Most of the animals in this group are univalves, meaning they have only one shell. Gastropods are the largest class of mollusks.

In univalves, the mantle lines the shell and helps protect the animal's soft body. In some species, such as marginellas and cowries, the mantle extends beyond the shell and is shaped like a hood or cape, protecting the outside shell.

A typical univalve can feel, smell, and taste. It has a head with eyes, and a mouth with a file-like tongue called the radula, which has many rows of sharp, grinding teeth. All gastropods have a digestive system and a heart, and breathe through gills.

Most univalves crawl about on their large, muscular foot. Some have a horny or shelly operculum or "trap door" on the back of the foot. In case of danger, the animal withdraws into its shell and closes the opening with the operculum.

Univalves usually have a single spiral shell, with an opening called the mouth. The edges of the mouth are called lips. The shapes of these shells are extremely variable, ranging from a long, slender spiral to cap-shaped. Some gastropods have no shell at all.

Pelecypods (Bivalves). The word pelecypod means "hatchet-footed," and refers to the shape of the foot in these mollusks. This group, the second largest group of mollusks, contains the two-shelled animals known as bivalves. In bivalves, the two shells or valves are joined by a hinge. Most bivalves push themselves along with a thick, muscular foot. They also use their foot to burrow. Some glue themselves to solid surfaces, while others fasten themselves to rocks and other solid surfaces with byssal threads. A few, such as some species of piddocks (p. 55), bore into solids. Some species seldom or never move; others swim, propelling themselves by means of water jets.

The mantle lines the two shell halves. Some bivalves have nerves along the edge of the mantle. In scallops and thorny oysters, these nerves end in light-sensitive, primitive "eyes." In some clams, the mantle is rolled into a pair of tubes that serve as siphons. Bivalves have two siphon tubes. An inhale siphon draws in sea water, carrying with it oxygen and bits of food. The exhale siphon carries out excess water and body wastes. Siphons are long in soft-shell clams and other bivalves that burrow.

Bivalves have no head and no radular teeth, just a mouth opening. They filter their food, algae, out of the water with their gills. All bivalves have a heart, nervous system, and digestive system.

5

Some kinds of bivalves are hermaphroditic, meaning they have both male and female sex organs in the same body, but in most species the sexes are separate — an individual is male or female, not both.

Scaphopods (Tusk Shells). The name scaphopod means "plow-footed." These tusk-shaped mollusks live partially buried in mud or sand. Their shells are tubes, open at both ends. Sea water is drawn in the small end, flushing the mantle with oxygen, and is shot out the larger end. Tusk shells have no gills — they "breathe" by absorbing oxygen through the mantle skin that lines the shell.

Sticking out of the large end of the shell is a tough, wormlike foot with a plow-shaped end, which is used for digging and burrowing. Dozens of bulb-tipped, hairlike threads called captaculae anchor the tusk in the sand. These threads also seize and bring the tiny, single-celled animals on which the mollusk feeds to its mouth.

Scaphopods have a mouth with file-like radular teeth and a digestive system, but no heart. The sexes are separate.

Cephalopods (Octopods, Squids, and Others). The name of this group of mollusks, derived from a word meaning "head-foot," refers to the eight or more arms coming out of the head and surrounding the mouth. This class includes the Octopus, Squid, Cuttlefish, Spirula, Chambered Nautilus, and the Argonauts. All species are carnivores (meat-eaters). They feed on other animals, such as fish, snails, and crabs, using their parrot-like beak and the radula.

Cephalopods have large, highly developed eyes. Their keen vision, combined with a quick, responsive brain and nervous system, allows them to be swift and alert. Many cephalopods, such as the Squid, can move fast by drawing water into the mantle cavity of the body and forcing it out through a tubular funnel (see p. 64). The force of the water leaving the funnel causes their body to shoot through the water backward, with their arms trailing behind. The funnel is highly mobile and can be directed forward or backward for a quick change of direction.

All cephalopods have three hearts, one main one and two smaller ones, and their blood is blue. Octopods and squids can camouflage themselves by changing color quickly, and by giving off an inky "smoke screen" that clouds the water just long enough to allow them to hide or escape from their enemies.

Amphineura (Chitons). These mollusks range widely in size, from 1/3 of an inch to 13 inches or more. All of the animals in this primitive group of mollusks have a shell made up of eight separate and overlapping plates, held together by a tough, elastic girdle. A chiton's shell has tiny holes or pores that contain nerves, which in some species end in light-sensitive "eyes."

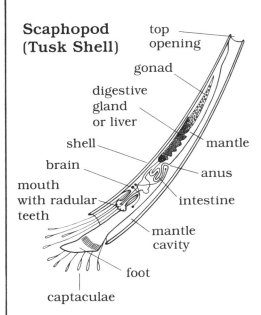

Scaphopod (Tusk Shell)

top opening

gonad

digestive gland or liver

shell

brain

mouth with radular teeth

mantle

anus

intestine

mantle cavity

foot

captaculae

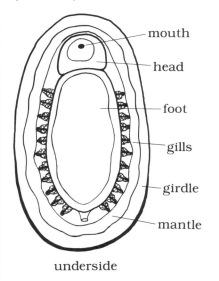

Amphineura (Chiton)

mouth

head

foot

gills

girdle

mantle

underside

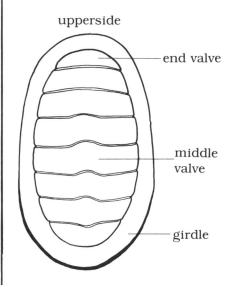

upperside

end valve

middle valve

girdle

Chitons have a mouth, with a file-like radula. They have a simple digestive system, a pair of kidneys, a heart, a nervous system, and gills.

A large, broad, muscular foot allows chitons to attach themselves with great suction to rocks, and also lets them move about. These mollusks feed at night on algae. When disturbed, chitons can roll themselves up in a ball, like an armadillo. The sexes are separate.

Collecting Shells

The sea is not the only place where we can find shells — they are found everywhere in the world, from the Himalayan mountains to deserts and jungles. You can find living mollusks in oceans, rivers, streams, lakes, ponds, tidal pools, and swamps, and fossilized ones in rocks or stone walls. You may even find shells in your own backyard or garden.

Going out to hunt for shells is an adventure with rewards. If you are at a beach after a storm, you could find shells that have washed ashore from deeper water, maybe even a rare one. At low tide, you can walk on an area that is usually covered with water. Clams are easy to spot — look for little bubbles or squirts of water coming up out of the sand. You'll need a shovel to dig up the clam. If you're going to dig up more than one, check to see whether you'll need a permit.

Most mollusks are night-feeders, so go to the beach at night and take a flashlight. Look for them at low tide, and check under rocks and on seaweed.

Wear shoes to protect your feet while you're wading. You'll even need gloves occasionally. A glass-bottom bucket will help you search the bottom in shallow water. In deeper water, take along a snorkel, a face mask, some swim fins, a cloth or mesh bag for your specimens, and most important of all, a "buddy" for safety. You'll also need digging and prying tools and perhaps a bucket for keeping aquarium specimens alive in sea water. Rare, deepwater specimens are occasionally brought up by dredging in deep water; some also turn up in the bellies of fish.

Don't put paint, varnish, or oil on shells — it takes away from their natural beauty. A brush will get the surface of the shell clean. If you find a shell that contains a smelly, partially rotten dead mollusk, you might have to bury it for a while. Let insects do the job of cleaning the shell for you.

When collecting, don't get carried away. Take at most only three of each kind: one to keep, one to trade, and one to give away. Broken shells are good to collect until you can replace them with better ones later.

Lastly, label your shells. Record what kind they are, and when and where you found them. New species are found all the time. If you are the first to discover one, you could even have it named after you!

Jackie Leatherbury Douglass

Atlantic Carrier Shell

upperside

underside

The animal that lives in this shell cements various bits of shells, stones, and coral to its shell for camouflage.

Queen Conch

Rooster-tail
Conch

Florida
Crown Conch

Florida
Fighting Conch

Conch or Stromb Shells

These thick, solid shells have a notch called the stromboid notch near the lower end. Conch snails "walk" by stabbing their sharp, thorny trap door or operculum into the sand and rolling over. These large carnivores (meat-eaters) live mostly in shallow grassy areas of warm seas.

Queen Conch
This shell, shown on the cover, is also known as the Pink Conch and the Queen Stromb. Color the outside peachy buff and cream, and the inside bright rosy pink. The mollusk, which is good to eat, occasionally produces pink pearls. Besides being used for doorstops and decorations, these shells are cut into cameos, and the scraps are ground into a powder that is used in manufacturing porcelain. Shell 8 to 12 in. high; found in shallow water from southern Florida to the West Indies. (1)

Rooster-tail Conch
This shell is also known as the Cock Stromb. The outside is white, with orangish brown markings. Color the inside light purple to peachy white. Shell 4 to 7 in. high; found from southeastern Florida to the West Indies. (2)

Florida Fighting Conch
Also called the Florida Stromb. Color the outside brown on a peachy white background, with orange and purple markings. The inside is white, shading to red-orange and purple-brown on the lip. The inside is a paler whitish color. Shell 2¾ to 5 in. high; found from North Carolina to Texas. (3)

Florida Crown Conch
This conch shell is dark brown to purple-brown on the outside, with tan and white stripes. Shell 1 to 8 in. high; found from Florida to the Gulf states and Mexico. (4)

Milk Conch
This shell is also called the Ribbed Stromb. Color the outside yellowish white and the inside a shiny cream color. Shell 4 to 7 in. high; found in shallow water from Florida to the West Indies. (5)

Hawk-wing Conch
The outside of this conch shell is brown and gray, with peachy white spots. The inside is pink, becoming white at the outside edge. Shell 4 to 6 in. high; found from southeastern Florida to Brazil. (6)

West Indian Fighting Conch
This shell is also called the Fighting Stromb. It is a deep yellow-brown, with paler bands. Make the inside bright red-orange to peach. Shell 3 to 5 in. high; found from southern Florida to Brazil. (7)

Milk Conch

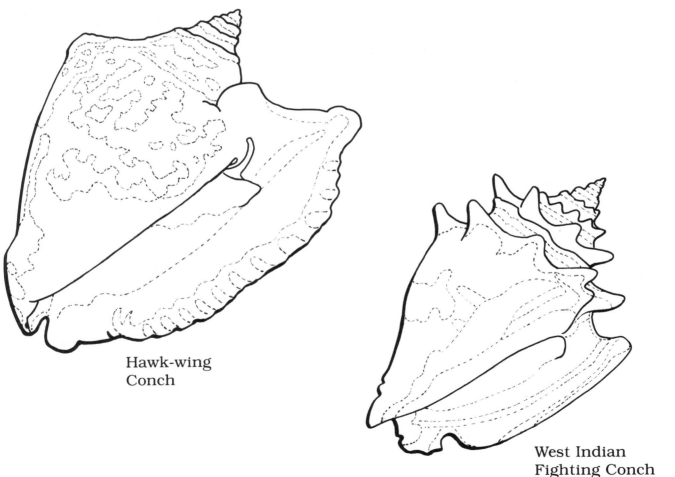

Hawk-wing
Conch

West Indian
Fighting Conch

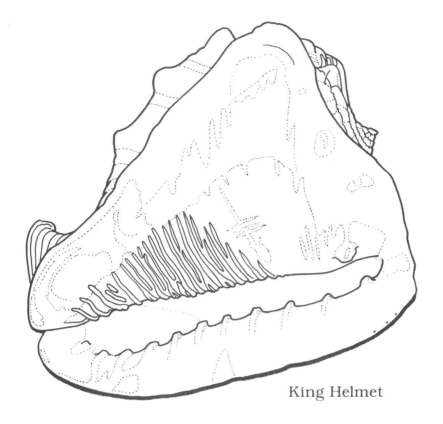

King Helmet

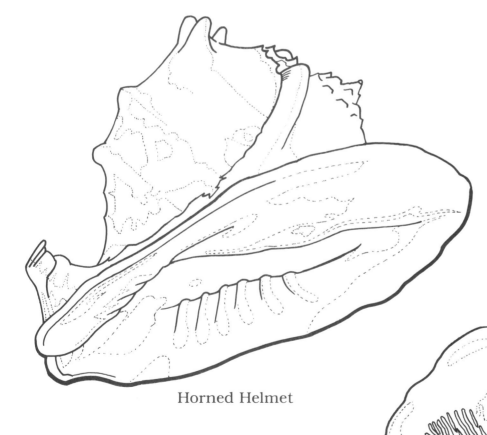

Horned Helmet

Helmet Shells

Helmet shells are found in warm water, in the Pacific Ocean and from Florida to Brazil. These mollusks creep over the sand and feed on sea urchins and sand dollars. The meat of helmet snails is used to make chowder, and their heavy, smooth shells are used as trumpets, cameo jewelry, and doorstops. South Pacific islanders use halved helmet shells as cooking pots and boat bailers.

King Helmet
This shell's outer lip is peach-colored, with brown and reddish brown patches. The teeth along the lip are white. The outside of the shell is gray, with tan streaks. Shell 4 to 9 in. high; found in shallow water from North Carolina to Brazil. (8)

Flame Helmet
Color the outer lip of this shell yellowish, with brown and gray patches. Unlike some other species of helmet shells, this one has no brown spots between the teeth on the bottom lip. The outside has shades of brown and gray. Shell 3 to 6 in. high; found in shallow water from southern Florida to Brazil. (9)

Horned Helmet
This shell is grayish white, marked with brown. The outer lip is a rich yellow-orange. Shell up to 12 in. high; found in deep water around Hawaii. (10)

Flame Helmet

Scotch Bonnet
This shell is pale yellow, with
reddish brown to orange spots.
It is 1 to 3⅝ in. high, and
found on sand in shallow water
from North Carolina through
the West Indies to Brazil. This
helmet shell is the official state
shell of North Carolina. (11)

Atlantic Partridge Tun
Color the outside of this thin
shell light brown, with darker
brown and white spots. The inside is tan, with a white lip.
Shell 2 to 5¼ in. high; found in
sand in shallow water, from
southeastern Florida to Brazil.
(12)

Smooth Scotch Bonnet
Similar to the Scotch Bonnet,
but without spiral grooves.
This shell is less solid and has
a thinner outer lip. The outside
is pale yellow with brown spots.
The inside is yellow, the lip
white. Shell 1½ to 2 in. high;
found in moderately shallow
water, from Bermuda and
southern Florida to the West Indies. (13)

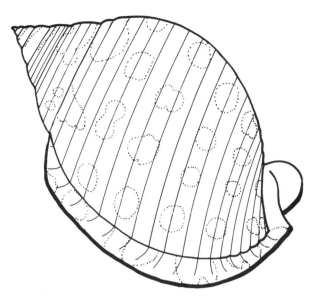

Scotch Bonnet

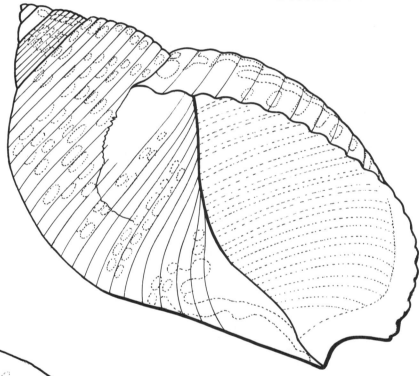

Atlantic
Partridge Tun

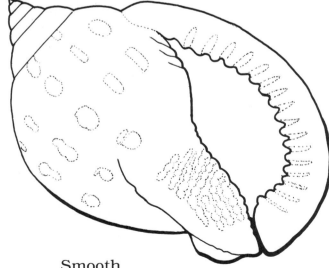

Smooth
Scotch Bonnet

11

Frog Shells

Frog shells have a ridge that runs from the top of the opening to the top of the shell. The mollusks are carnivores (meat-eaters).

St. Thomas Frog Shell
Color the outside lavender or grayish white, with reddish brown spots. The inside is lavender. Shell ½ to 1¼ in. high. Found under rocks and coral, on reefs in shallow warm water from North Carolina to Brazil. (14)

California Frog Shell
The outside of this frog shell is yellowish brown. The inside is white, with a grayish brown lip. Shell 1½ to 5 in. high; found in shallow water from California to Baja California. (15)

Chestnut Frog Shell
The outside is yellowish brown, marked with orange-brown. Color the inside a very pale lavender. A rare shell, 1 to 2 in. high. Found in moderately deep water from southern Florida to the West Indies. (16)

Corrugated Frog Shell
This shell is also called the Gaudy Frog Shell. Color the outside buff, with tan and orange markings and purple-brown spots. Inside, the lip is yellow-orange to pale lavender. Shell 2 to 3 in. high. Found in southeastern Florida and farther south in the western Atlantic, and from California to Ecuador in the eastern Pacific. (17)

St. Thomas
Frog Shell

California
Frog Shell

Corrugated
Frog Shell

Chestnut
Frog Shell

Whelk Shells

Whelks have a long, tubular extension of their head called a proboscis, which has a mouth on the end. They eat decaying plant and animal material.

Knobbed Whelk
Color the outside a peachy white; the inside, a deep orange. Shell 4 to 9 in. high; found in shallow water from Massachusetts to Florida. (18)

Turnip Whelk
The outside is buffy gray, with purplish brown streaks. The inside is yellow-orange. Shell 5 to 6 in. high; found in shallow water in the Gulf of Mexico. (19)

Lightning Whelk
Color the outside of this shell peach, with violet-brown streaks. The inside is white to peachy white. Shell 3 to 5 in. high; found from North Carolina to Florida and westward to Texas. (20)

Pear Whelk
This whelk shell is peachy white on the outside, with orange-brown streaks. Inside, it is whitish, with orangish blotches. Shell 2½ to 5½ in. high; found from North Carolina to Mexico. (21)

Common Fig Shell
Fig shells are sand-dwellers with a wide, flat foot. This fig shell is light peach, with a lavender-gray tinge both inside and out. Shell 2½ to 5 in. high; found in sand, in shallow water from North Carolina to Mexico. (22)

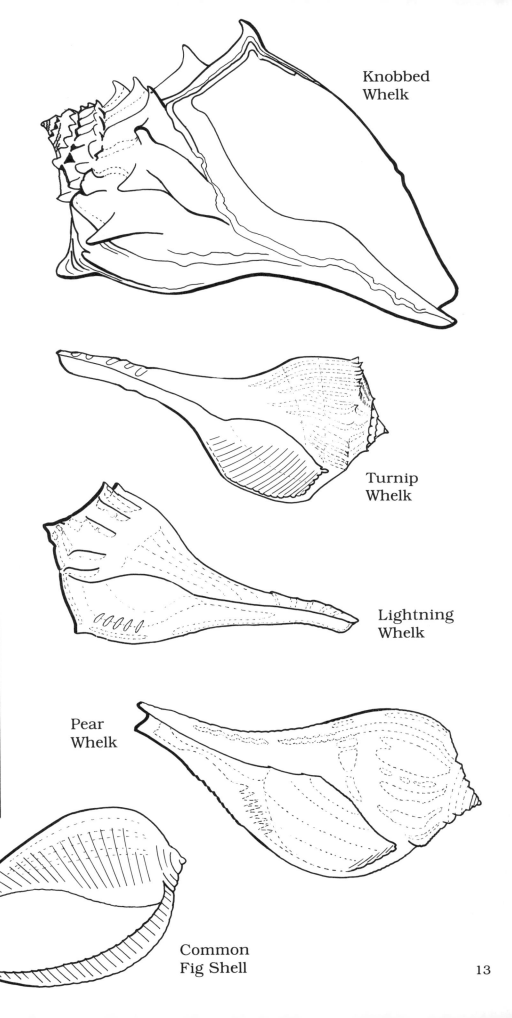

Knobbed Whelk

Turnip Whelk

Lightning Whelk

Pear Whelk

Common Fig Shell

13

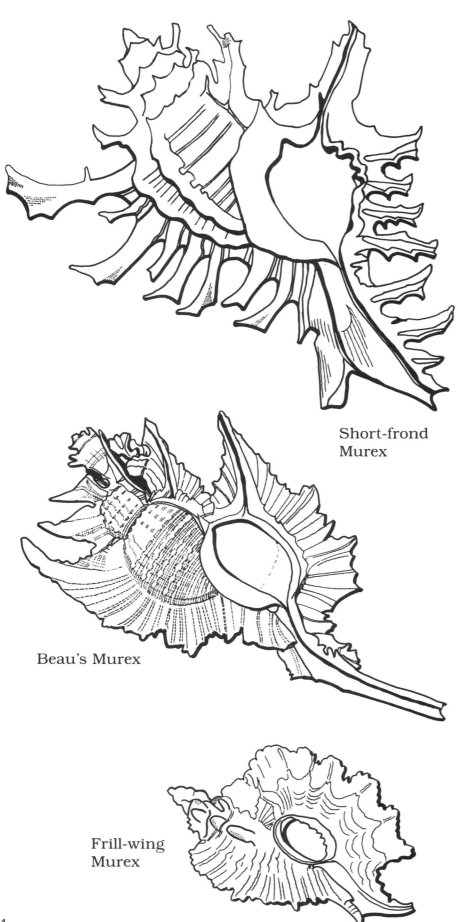

Short-frond
Murex

Beau's Murex

Frill-wing
Murex

Murex Shells

Murex shells are thick and spiny. They are found world-wide in tropical waters, on rocks or reefs. Murex snails are carnivores. They bore into clam shells using a rasplike "tongue" called the radula and pry the shell open with their foot, aided by the long tooth at the base of the outer lip, plus the suction of their foot. When threatened, these snails produce a yellowish liquid that smells like garlic. When exposed to sunlight, this liquid becomes the royal purple dye that was treasured by the ancient Phoenicians and the Romans.

Short-frond Murex
This shell is also called the West Indian Murex. Color the outside yellowish white to pale brown, with spiral lines that are stained dark brown. The spines are paler brown. The inside is white. Shell 3 to 6 in. high; found in shallow water from southern Florida to the West Indies. (23)

Beau's Murex
The outside of this shell is creamy yellow, with touches of brown. The inside is white. A rare shell, 3 to 4 in. high. Found in deep water from southern Florida to the West Indies. (24)

Frill-wing Murex
The shell of this murex is the color of brown sugar, with white around the opening. Shell 1¾ to 2¾ in. high; found on rocks at the low-tide line, from California to Baja California. (25)

Pink-mouthed Murex
This shell is pinkish white on the outside and rosy pink on the inside. Shell 3 to 6 in. high; found in moderately shallow water from the Gulf of California to Peru. (26)

Hexagonal Murex
The outside of this murex shell is white, tinged with pinkish brown. The inside is yellowish pink. Shell 1 to 1⅝ in. high; found under rocks, on reefs from the Florida Keys to the West Indies. (27)

Cabrit's Murex
This murex shell has yellowish pink markings on a white background. Shell 1 to 3 in. high; found on sandy bottoms in shallow to deep water, from South Carolina to the West Indies. (28)

Catalina Trophon
The outside of this shell is yellowish brown, with darker tones in the shadows. The inside is white, with a brown and yellow trap door. Shell 3 to 4 in. high; found in deep water in southern California. (29)

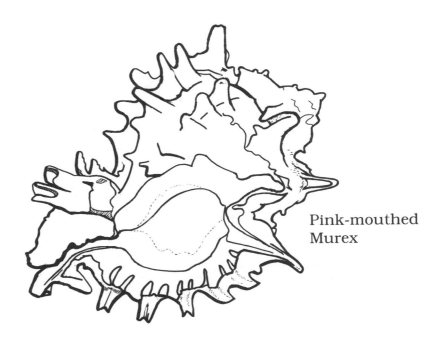

Pink-mouthed Murex

Hexagonal Murex

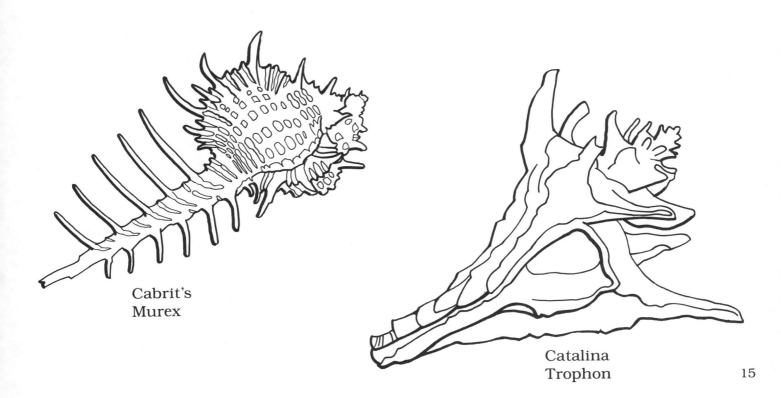

Cabrit's Murex

Catalina Trophon

15

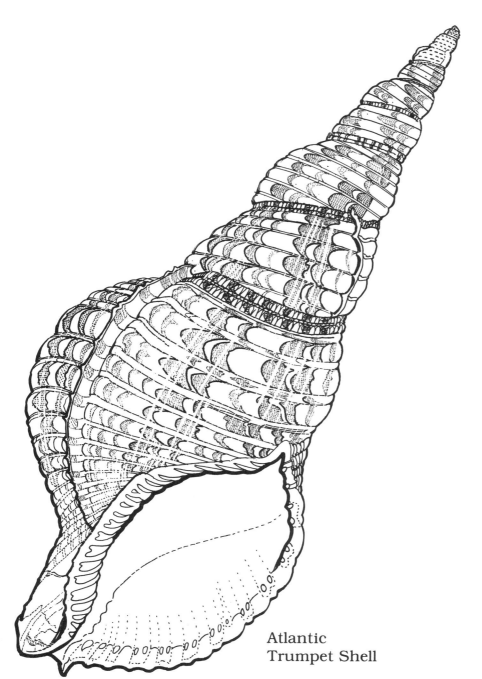

Atlantic
Trumpet Shell

Triton Shells

Tritons are found in warm and temperate waters worldwide. The larvae (young) take several months to develop into adults and drift for long distances, which accounts for their wide distribution. Nearly all tritons grow a spiny, hairy outer covering on the shell that protects them from predators. Tritons feed on other mollusks, both snails and clams. First they render their prey helpless by secreting a paralyzing fluid, then they insert their mouth part into the shell to feed on the soft parts of their prey. The larger triton shells have been used as trumpets since ancient times.

Atlantic Trumpet Shell
Also called Triton's Trumpet. Color the outside of this triton shell purplish brown, with shades of tan and white. The inside is pale orange. Shell 10 to 15 in. high; found in moderately shallow water from southern Florida to the West Indies. (30)

Gold-mouthed Triton
This shell is grayish white on the outside, mottled with brown. Inside, it is pale orange with white teeth. Shell 2 to 3 in. high; found on reefs, in shallow water from Florida to Brazil. (31)

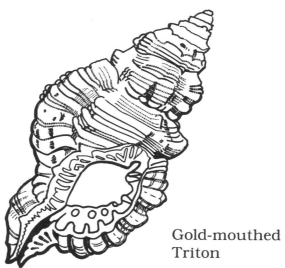

Gold-mouthed
Triton

Frilled Dogwinkle
Color this shell a rich shade of yellow-brown. Shell 1 to 3¼ in. high; found on rocks below the low-tide line, from Alaska to California. (32)

Mauve-mouthed Drill
This shell is a grayish orchid color on the outside and lavender pink on the inside. Shell ¾ to 1¼ in. high; found on rocks from the low-tide line to deep water, from western Florida to the Florida Keys. (33)

Atlantic Distorsio
The outside is white, with yellowish brown, yellow, and orange markings. The inside is white, but looks brownish gray in shadow. Shell ¾ to 3½ in. high; found on sand among coral and rocks, from North Carolina to Brazil. (34)

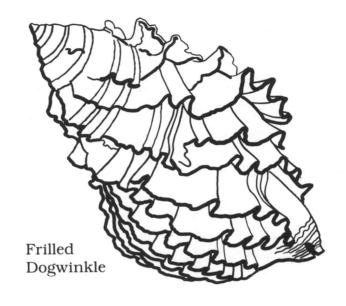

Frilled
Dogwinkle

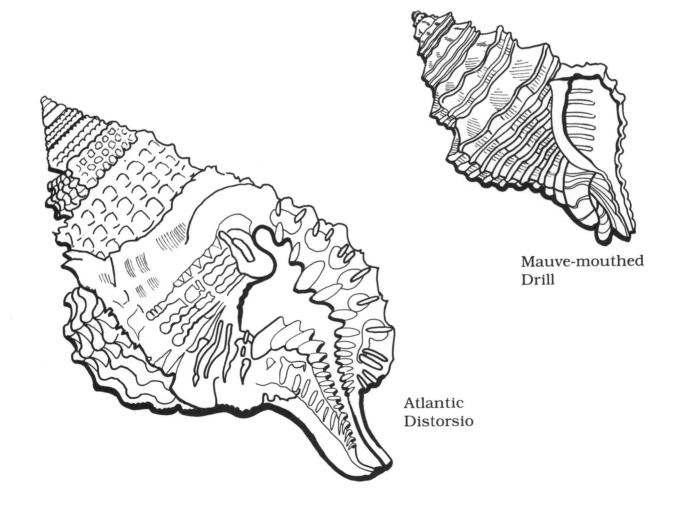

Mauve-mouthed
Drill

Atlantic
Distorsio

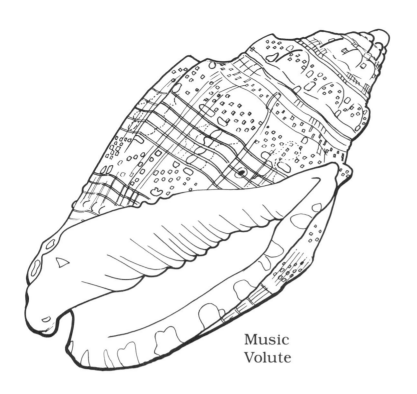

Music
Volute

Volute Shells

The collector's favorite! Volutes have thick, shiny, spiraled shells that come in an elaborate assortment of patterns and colors. They are found in deep water in tropical seas.

Music Volute
The outside is peachy pink, with reddish brown and gray lines and spots that suggest musical "notes." Inside, the lip is rosy peach, with dark brown spots. Shell 2 to 2½ in. high; found from the West Indies to South America. (35)

Dubious Volute
A peachy pink shell with chocolate brown spots. The inside is peach-colored. A rare shell, 2 in. high; found in southern Florida. (36)

Dohrn's Volute
Color this shell cream on the outside with chocolate brown spots, and cream on the inside. Another rare shell found in southern Florida; 2 to 3 in. high. (37)

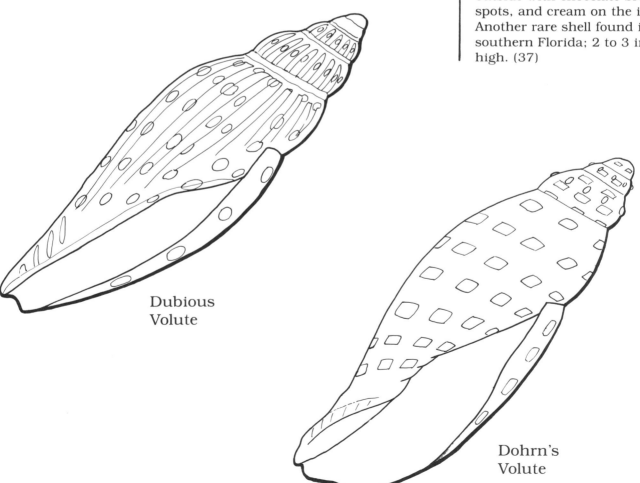

Dubious
Volute

Dohrn's
Volute

18

Junonia

This shell is also called Juno's Volute. The outside is pinkish white, with chocolate brown spots. The inside is cream. Shell 3 to 6 in. high; found in moderately deep water from South Carolina to the Gulf of Mexico. (38)

Johnstone's Junonia

Color the outside apricot, with dark brown spots. Make the inside a lighter gold. This mollusk is closely related to Junonia. Shell 3 to 6 in. high; found in deep water off the coasts of Alabama and Mississippi. (39)

Florida Volute

A yellowish gray volute shell, with brownish spots. Shell 3 to 4 in. high; found in deep water off the Florida Keys. (40)

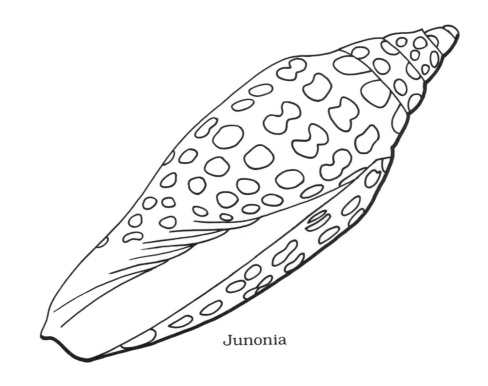

Junonia

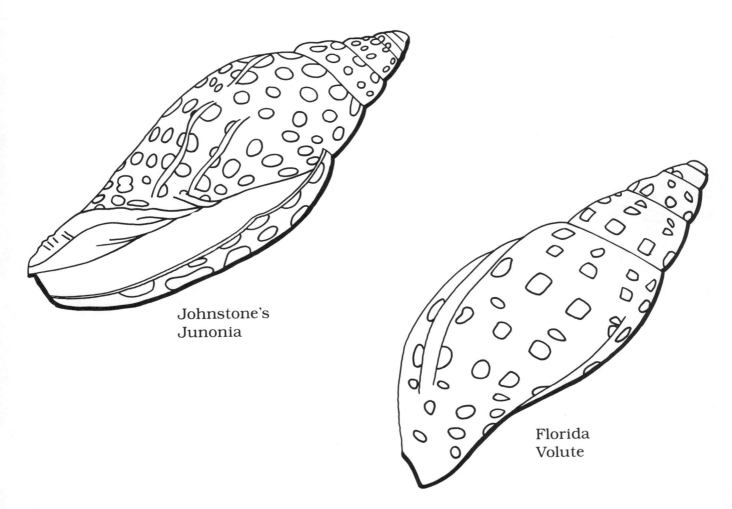

Johnstone's
Junonia

Florida
Volute

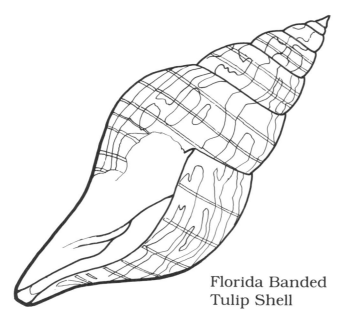

Florida Banded
Tulip Shell

Tulip Shells

These are the largest uni-valves (single-shelled mollusks) in American waters. The Giant Band Shell or Florida Horse Conch grows up to 2 ft. long. Tulip conchs are aggressive, carnivorous mollusks that feed on other snails and clams. These shells are found in shallow water in warm seas.

Florida Banded Tulip Shell
The outside of this shell is purple, green, gold, and bluish gray with white, cloudy markings and dark brown lines. The inside is white, but the outside colors show through. 2 to 4 in. high; found from North Carolina to Florida and the Gulf states. (41)

True Tulip Shell
Color the outside pinkish gray to red-orange, streaked with reddish brown and gold. The inside is transparent white. Shell 4 to 6 in. high; found from North Carolina to the West Indies. (42)

Banded Tulip Shell
Color this shell grayish yellow, with orange streaks and fine reddish brown lines. Shell 2¼ to 4⅛ in. high; found from Florida to Mexico. (43)

True
Tulip Shell

Banded
Tulip Shell

Miter Shells

These solid, thick shells are often brilliantly colored. They come in both sculptured and smooth forms, and are very popular with collectors. Miter snails live mainly in warm seas. They usually feed at night on clams and marine worms. Some species give off a smelly purple fluid when disturbed.

Royal Florida Miter
The outside of this shell is white, with orange-brown dots. The inside is white. A rare shell, 1½ to 2 in. high. Found from southern Florida to the West Indies. (44)

Ida's Miter
Color this shell brownish purple inside and out. Shell 2½ in. high; found in shallow water in southern California. (45)

Henderson's Miter
This tiny shell is grayish white on the outside, with orange-tan bands. The inside is tan. Shell ¼ in. high, found from southeastern Florida to the Caribbean. (46)

Barbados Miter
A yellowish brown miter shell, with white spots. The inside is brown. Shell 1 to 1¾ in. high; found from southeastern Florida to Brazil. (47)

Sulcate Miter
Both inside and out, this shell is dark brown with paler bands. Shell 1 in. high; found from North Carolina to the West Indies. (48)

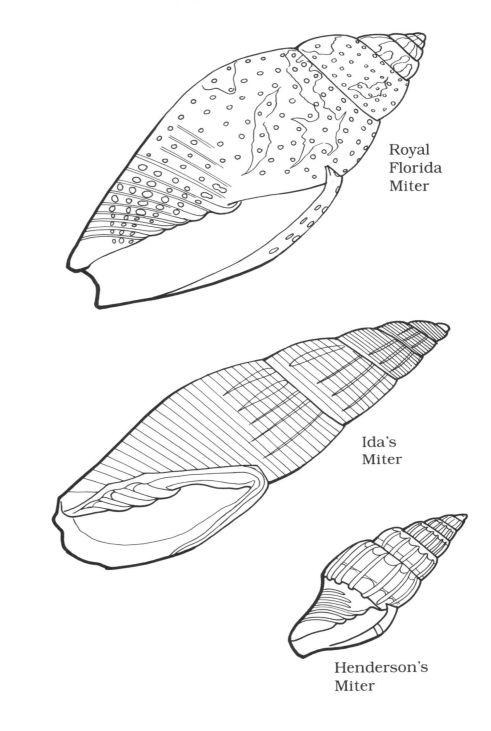

Royal Florida Miter

Ida's Miter

Henderson's Miter

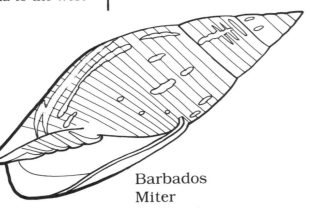

Barbados Miter

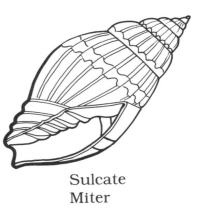

Sulcate Miter

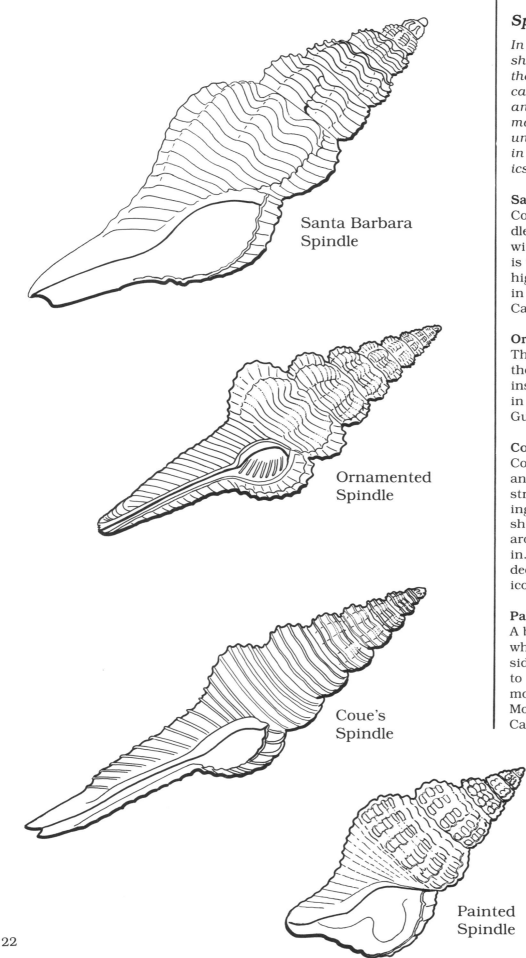

Santa Barbara
Spindle

Ornamented
Spindle

Coue's
Spindle

Painted
Spindle

Spindle Shells

In these heavy, spindle-shaped shells, the opening at the base ends in a long, open canal. The snails are slow and deliberate. They feed on marine worms, and eat both univalves and bivalves. Found in pairs, on sand in the tropics.

Santa Barbara Spindle
Color the outside of this spindle shell yellowish white, tinged with reddish brown. The inside is white. Shell 2¼ to 5¼ in. high; found on sand or rocks, in deep water from Oregon to California. (49)

Ornamented Spindle
This shell is orangish white on the outside, and white on the inside. Shell 3 in. high; found in moderately deep water in the Gulf of Mexico. (50)

Coue's Spindle
Coue's Spindle is white inside and out, with a yellowish tan streak around the canal opening. It is named for the French ship's captain who discovered it around 1855. Shell 2¼ to 4½ in. high; found on sand, in deep water in the Gulf of Mexico. (51)

Painted Spindle
A brown shell, with yellowish white, spiraling bands. The inside is tan and brown. Shell ½ to 1 in. high; found on sand in moderately deep water from Monterey, California to Baja California. (52)

Turrid Shells

This is the largest family of mollusks; it evolved over 100 million years ago. The shell's outer lip has a characteristic notch, called the "turrid notch." The snails in this group live in deep water, in temperate seas throughout the world.

White Giant Turrid
A white shell, 2½ to 5 in. high. It is found from North Carolina to the West Indies. (53)

Oyster Turrid
Color this shell orangish brown inside and out. Shell ½ to 1 in. high; found from North Carolina to the Virgin Islands. (54)

Perverse Turrid
The shell of this turrid snail is "left-handed" — it spirals to the left as the animal grows. Shell 1½ to 2 in. high; found from Alaska to southern California. (55)

Carpenter's Turrid
Color the outside of this shell golden brown, with light streaks and reddish brown bands. The inside is peach. Shell 1¾ to 3¾ in. high; found from central California to Baja California. (56)

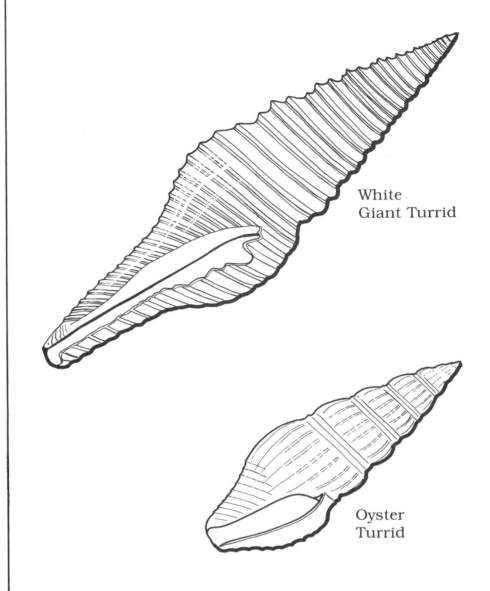

White
Giant Turrid

Oyster
Turrid

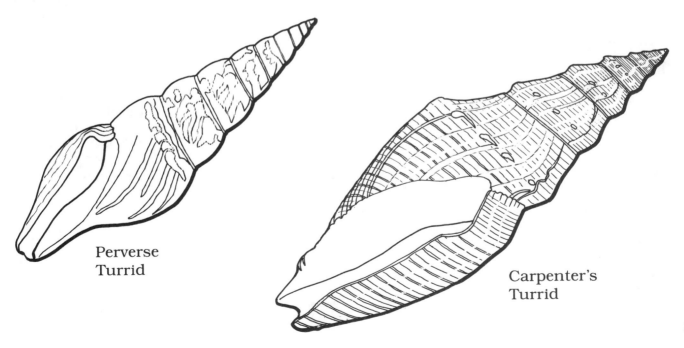

Perverse
Turrid

Carpenter's
Turrid

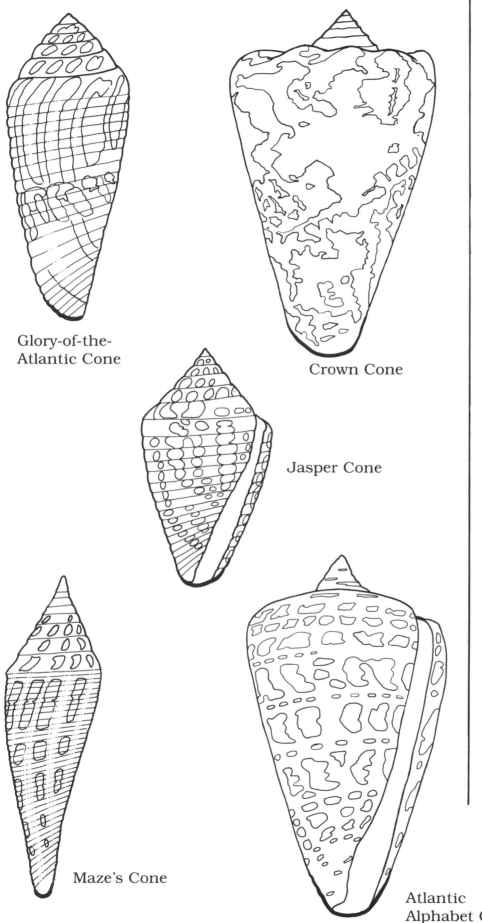

Glory-of-the-
Atlantic Cone

Crown Cone

Jasper Cone

Maze's Cone

Atlantic
Alphabet Cone

Cone Shells

These beautiful, cone-shaped shells are smooth or have grooves. Rare ones sell for thousands of dollars. Cone snails produce a poison from a gland within their bodies. Although no deadly species occur in our area, all cone snails should be handled with extreme caution.

Glory-of-the-Atlantic Cone
A rosy pink to orange shell, with encircling spots of white and brown. An uncommon shell, 1 to 1¾ in. high. It is found in moderately deep water from southern Florida to the West Indies. (57)

Crown Cone
This cone shell is white, mottled with dark brown and yellowish red-brown splotches. Shell 1½ to 3 in. high; found on reefs from southern Florida to Brazil. (58)

Jasper Cone
The outside of this shell is white, marked with orange. The inside is white. Shell ½ to 1 in. high; found in shallow water from southern Florida to Brazil. (59)

Maze's Cone
Color this cone shell yellowish tan, with orange-brown spots. A rare shell, 1½ to 2 in. high. Found in deep water from the Florida Keys to Brazil. (60)

Atlantic Alphabet Cone
A white shell, with yellow-orange spots on the outside. The inside is white. Shell 1¾ to 3 in. high; found in shallow water from Florida to Mexico. (61)

Carrot Cone
Color the outside of this cone shell carrot-orange, with a yellowish central band. Make the inside orange. A 2 in. high shell, found in moderately deep water from Florida to the West Indies. (62)

California Cone
This shell is reddish brown on the outside and brown on the inside. Shell ¾ to 1½ in. high; found in shallow water from California to Baja California. (63)

Florida Cone
A whitish shell with patches of orange on yellow-green bands; one band below the middle is white. Shell 1 to 2 in. high; found in deep water from North Carolina to Florida. (64)

Sozon's Cone
A rich orange cone shell with a pair of white bands around the middle. Red-brown dots cover the shell. 2 to 4 in. high; found in deep water from South Carolina to the Gulf of Mexico. (65)

Golden-banded Cone
Color the outside of this shell reddish brown, with light yellow bands. The inside is white with orange blotches. Shell 2 to 3 in. high; found in moderately deep water from the Florida Keys to Yucatan. (66)

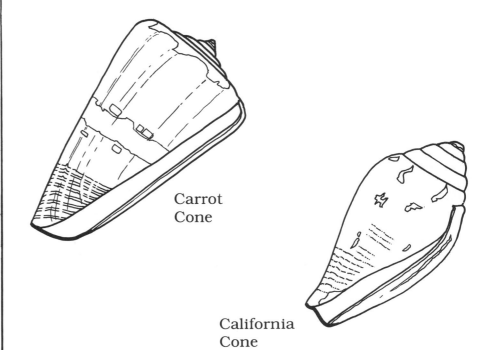

Carrot Cone

California Cone

Florida Cone

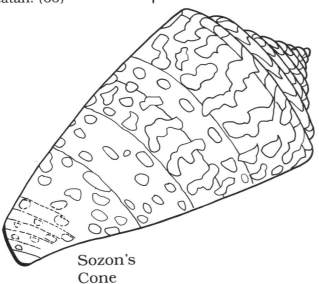

Sozon's Cone

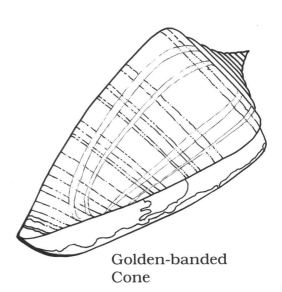

Golden-banded Cone

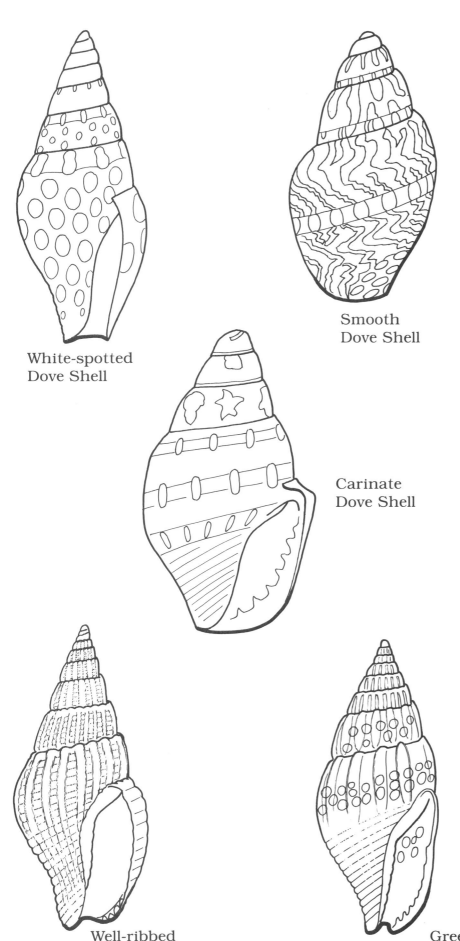

White-spotted
Dove Shell

Smooth
Dove Shell

Carinate
Dove Shell

Well-ribbed
Dove Shell

Greedy
Dove Shell

Dove Shells

The snails that live in dove shells are herbivores (vegetarians) that feed on algae. They are found worldwide. Most live on rocks, mud, or sand in shallow water. The color of these little shells is variable.

White-spotted Dove Shell
A dark brown dove shell with white spots. The inside is whitish brown. Shell ⅜ to ½ in. high; found from southeastern Florida to northern Brazil. (67)

Smooth Dove Shell
This dove shell is white, with yellow-orange zigzag streaks and red-brown bands with white dots. Shell ½ to ¾ in. high; found from the Florida Keys to the West Indies. (68)

Carinate Dove Shell
This shell has a purplish top and an apricot bottom, both with orange streaks, blotches, and bands. Shell ¼ to ⅜ in. high; found from southern Alaska to Mexico. (69)

Well-ribbed Dove Shell
Make the outside of this shell brownish gray, banded with darker brown. The inside is gray. Shell ⅜ to ½ in. high; found from Massachusetts to Florida. (70)

Greedy Dove Shell
An orange shell with white spots and bands. The inside is white, with a red-orange lip. Shell ⅜ to ¾ in. high; found from Massachusetts to Florida. (71)

Auger Shells

Auger shells are long and narrow, with many "whorls" or "turns." The base of the inner lip is twisted. Some auger snails have hollow teeth with barbs at the end that secrete a mild poison from a gland, but the American species are not dangerous. These mollusks feed on marine worms and live in sand, in shallow tropical water.

Flame Auger
Our largest auger shell. Color the outside yellowish white, with orange-brown marks. The inside is tan. Shell 3¾ to 6¼ in. high; found from southeastern Florida to the West Indies. (72)

Gray Atlantic Auger
The outside of this velvety-looking shell is gray to purplish brown. Each "turn" has a narrow whitish band, and a broader reddish brown band below that. The inside is dark brown. Shell 1 to 2 in. high; found from southeastern Florida to Brazil. (73)

Sallé's Auger
This shell is grayish tan to purple-brown. A pale band encircles the top of each turn, and a broader reddish brown band lies below this pale band. The vertical "ribs" are white. The inside is brown. Shell ½ to 1½ in. high; found from North Carolina to Texas. (74)

Shiny Atlantic Auger
A peachy white auger shell, with the lower ⅔ of each turn colored orange-tan. The ribs are whitish. The inside is white. Shell 1 to 2 in. high; found from southeastern Florida to the West Indies. (75)

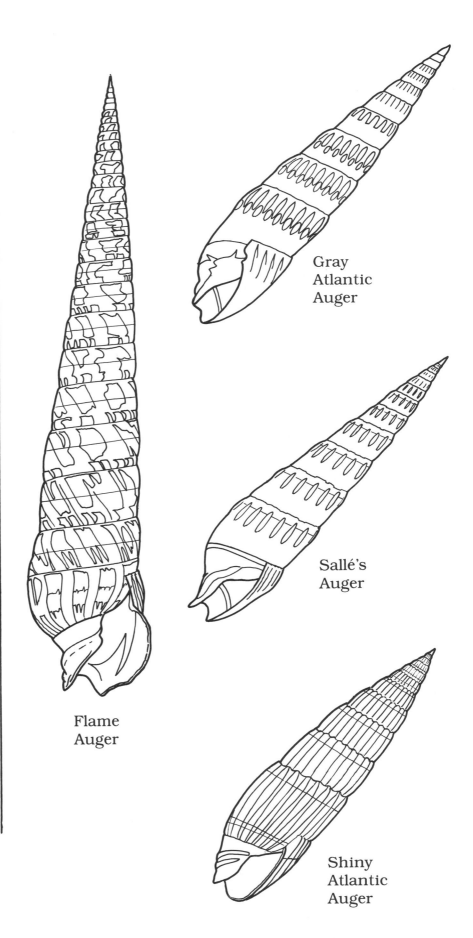

Gray Atlantic Auger

Sallé's Auger

Flame Auger

Shiny Atlantic Auger

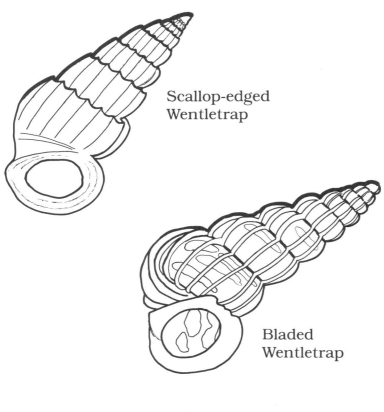

Scallop-edged
Wentletrap

Bladed
Wentletrap

Lamellose
Wentletrap

Krebs'
Wentletrap

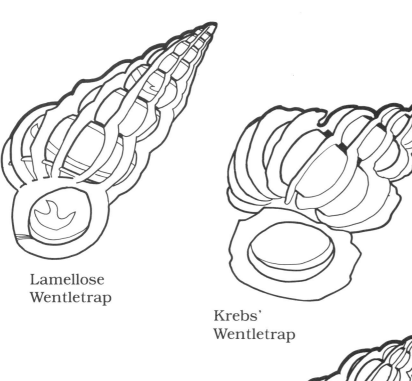

Angulate
Wentletrap

Wentletraps

A large family of small shells that are beautifully sculptured and usually white. Wentletrap is a Dutch word meaning "winding staircase." These "staircase shells" occur in all seas. Their delicately graceful shape makes them a favorite of shell collectors. Wentletrap snails are carnivores that feed on sea anemones and coral, tearing off big pieces with their large, file-like jaws. The animal exudes a pinkish purple dye when disturbed.

Scallop-edged Wentletrap
Also called the Sculptured Wentletrap. This shell is pinkish white. It is ⅜ to ¾ in. high, and is found on rocks at the low-tide line from southern California to Panama. (76)

Bladed Wentletrap
This shell is white, with light orangish tan marks. Shell ⅜ to ⅞ in. high; found in shallow water from southern Florida to Argentina. (77)

Lamellose Wentletrap
This shell is also called the Trellis Wentletrap. A white shell, with pinkish tan and pale brown markings. Shell ⅝ to 1¼ in. high; found in shallow water from southern Florida to West Africa. (78)

Krebs' Wentletrap
This white wentletrap is ⅜ to ¾ in. high. It is found in coral sand from South Carolina to Brazil. (79)

Angulate Wentletrap
One of the most common wentletraps. A white shell, ½ to ⅞ in. high; found in shallow water from New York to Florida and west to Texas. (80)

Top Shells

These spiral shells are usually shaped like pyramids, and are mostly made up of iridescent mother-of-pearl. All have a pearly inside. The snail's thorny, thin operculum is more or less round. These mollusks eat algae and are found in seaweed in shallow water, in warm and cold seas throughout the world.

Norris Top Shell
Color this shell chestnut brown, shading to darker brown near the opening. On one side of the opening is a blue-green, rounded edge called the columella. Shell 1¼ to 2¼ in. wide; found from California to Baja California. (81)

Superb Gaza Shell
A grayish yellow shell, with pink and green iridescent tints. Shell 1⅜ to 1½ in. wide; found from the West Indies to the Gulf of Mexico. (82)

West Indian Top Shell
Also called the Magpie Shell. Color the outside light yellowish gray, with purplish black splotches. Shell 2 to 4½ in. wide; found in the West Indies. (83)

Pacific Ringed Top Shell
Color the outside of this shell yellow, with pink bands. As in all top shells, the inside is pearly. Shell ⅝ to 1¼ in. high; found from southern Alaska to northern Baja California. (84)

Say's Top Shell
This shell is golden yellow, with rose bands. It is ⅝ to 1⅓ in. high, and is found from North Carolina to Florida. (85)

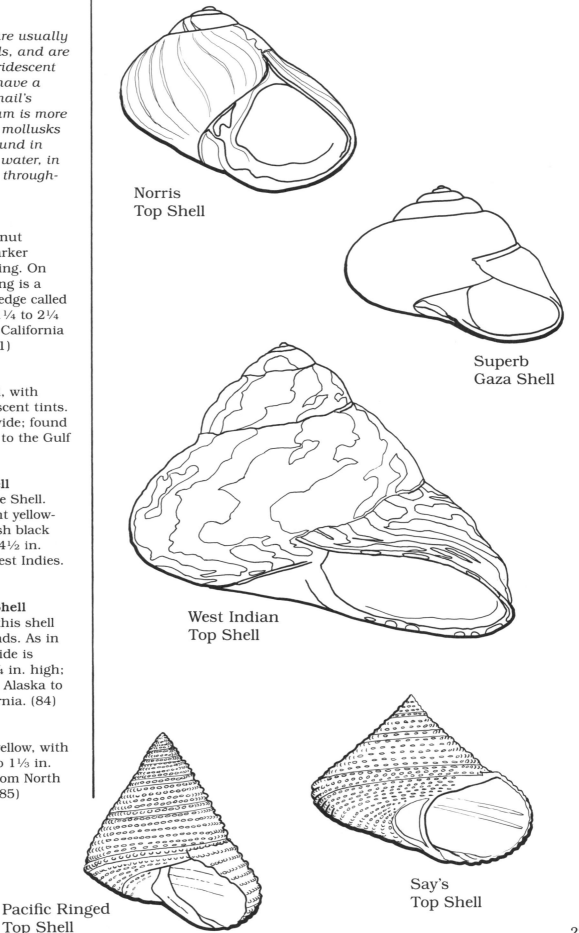

Norris
Top Shell

Superb
Gaza Shell

West Indian
Top Shell

Pacific Ringed
Top Shell

Say's
Top Shell

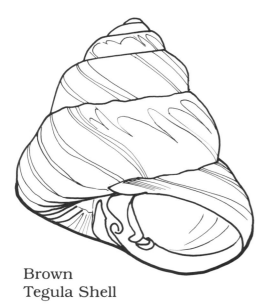

Brown
Tegula Shell

Tegula Shells

Tegula shells live on rocks and eat plants. These four species live among sea anemones, in cool water along the rocky coast of California.

Brown Tegula Shell
Color the outside orangish brown, with a tan base. The inside is pearly. Shell ¾ to 2 in. high. (86)

Queen Tegula Shell
A purplish and greenish gray shell, with a golden orange depression at the base. The inside is gold. Shell ¾ to 2 in. high. (87)

Speckled Tegula Shell
The outside of this shell is purplish black, with slanting golden stripes. The top, bottom, and inside are pearly. Shell ¾ to 1⅝ in. high. (88)

Gilded Tegula Shell
The outside of this shell is pea-greenish gray. A yellow-orange, crescent-shaped depression at the base is bordered by pale blue. The inside of the shell is pearly white. Shell ⅛ to 1 in. high. (89)

Queen
Tegula Shell

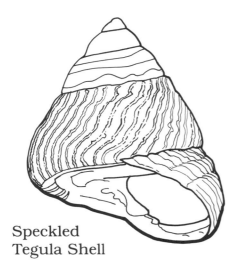

Speckled
Tegula Shell

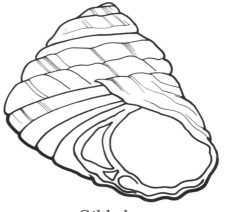

Gilded
Tegula Shell

Nerite Shells

These little jewels belong to a large tropical family inhabiting salty seas, brackish water, fresh water, and in some cases dry land. Some species are smooth, while others are strongly sculptured. Nerites live on rocks and feed on plants in the area between the high and low tide lines — the intertidal zone.

Zebra Nerite
This shell is black and white on the outside and golden yellow on the inside. Shell ⅜ to ½ in. high; found from southeastern Florida to the Caribbean. (90)

Emerald Nerite
Color the outside bright pea-green, with white dots. The inside is green. Shell ¼ in. high; found from Bermuda to Florida and south to Brazil. (91)

Virgin Nerite
This nerite shell comes in a large variety of colors. Make this one maroon, with white marks. The inside is usually yellow. Shell ¼ to ¾ in. high; found from Bermuda to Florida and south to Brazil. (92)

Polished Nerite
This nerite shell is also extremely variable in color. Give this one wide olive bands, with narrower red bands, both with peach-colored marks. Shell 1½ in. high; found along Hawaiian shores. (93)

Bleeding Tooth
Color the outside of this shell orangish yellow, with black and red zigzag markings. The teeth are white, surrounded by red-orange blotches. The inside is yellow. Shell ¾ to 1½ in. high; found from southeastern Florida to Brazil. (94)

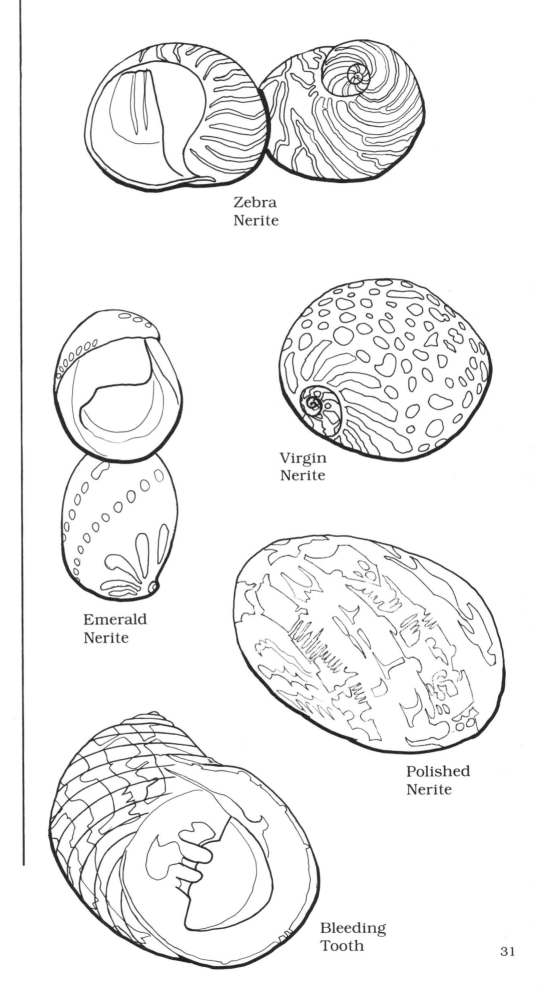

Zebra
Nerite

Virgin
Nerite

Emerald
Nerite

Polished
Nerite

Bleeding
Tooth

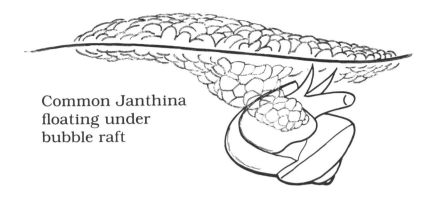

Common Janthina
floating under
bubble raft

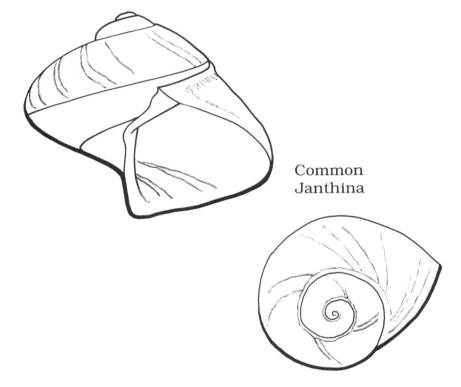

Common
Janthina

Janthina or Violet Shells

*Also known as purple snails,
these mollusks float on the
open sea, miles from land.
They cannot swim, but float in
colonies on the surface of
warm tropical seas throughout
the world. As shown in the
drawing, the animal produces
jellylike, lavender bubbles of
mucus and cements them to its
foot. The snail fastens its eggs
to the underside of this raft of
bubbles, and there they develop into young shellfish.*

*The extremely fragile shells
of the janthinas range in color
from pale lavender to deep
purple. The shell has no operculum, but the snail defends
itself by producing a purple
fluid when irritated. Janthina
snails are carnivores, feeding
mostly on jellyfish and other
animals they come upon in the
open sea.*

Common Janthina
The top of this shell is dark to
light lavender. The bottom is
deep purple. Shell 1 to 2½ in.
wide. (95)

Globe Janthina
Color this janthina shell evenly
violet all over. Shell ¾ to 1 in.
wide. (96)

Pallid Janthina
Color this shell pale pinkish
purple. It is 1½ in. wide. (97)

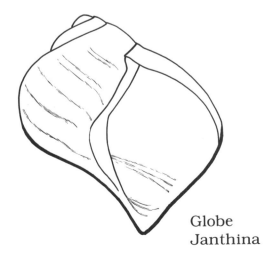

Globe
Janthina

Pallid
Janthina

Cowry Shells (Cowries)

A large group of highly polished, brilliantly colored shells with teeth on both lips. The snails live under rocks in the daytime and feed on algae at night. Cowries are found in all tropical seas and in the warmer waters along the North American coastline. These shells were once used as money in Africa and other regions. Fur traders bartered cowries to the North American Indians, who wore them as signs of wealth.

Atlantic Yellow Cowry
A yellow-orange cowry shell, with white and brown spots. Shell ¾ to 1¼ in. long; found from North Carolina to Brazil. (98)

Atlantic Gray Cowry
Color this shell cream, with purple-brown between some of the teeth. The sides are light brown. Shell ¾ to 1½ in. long; found from North Carolina to Brazil. (99)

Measled Cowry
Color this shell light tan, darker on the sides. It has white spots with brown centers. Shell 2 to 4½ in. long; found from southeastern Florida to Brazil. (100)

Chestnut Cowry
This shell has a peachy white edge. The center is orange-tan and brown, outlined with dark reddish brown. Shell 1 to 2½ in. long; found from central California to Baja California. (101)

Deer Cowry
A dark yellow-brown shell with white spots. It is 3½ to 5 in. long; found from southern Florida to the West Indies. (102)

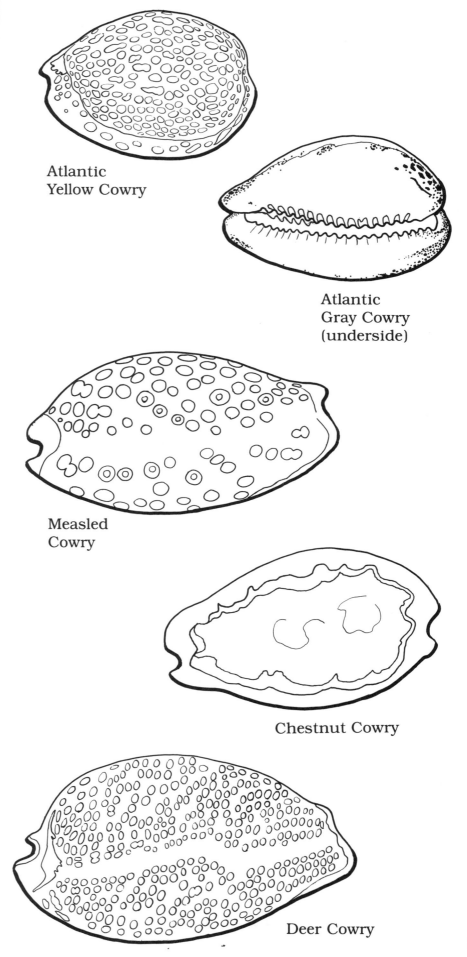

Atlantic
Yellow Cowry

Atlantic
Gray Cowry
(underside)

Measled
Cowry

Chestnut Cowry

Deer Cowry

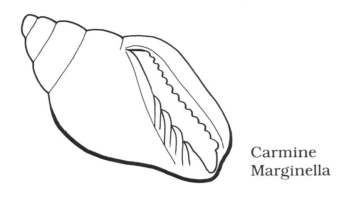

Carmine
Marginella

Tan
Marginella

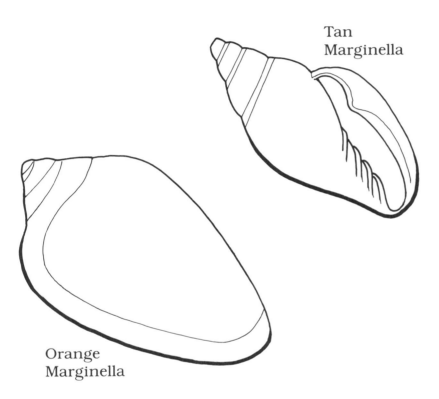

Orange
Marginella

Princess
Marginella

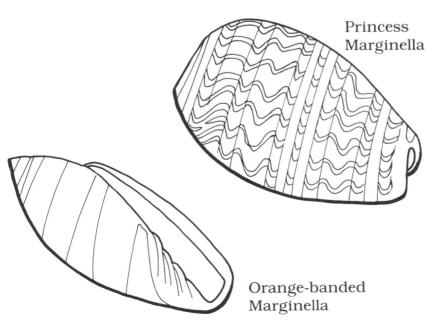

Orange-banded
Marginella

Marginellas

Smooth, shiny, brightly colored shells, marginellas are usually found in tropical and warm water. The outer lip is smooth and finely toothed, and has a thickened margin that gives the family its name. The snails are carnivores and live among algae, in sand or under stones. These porcelain-like shells were used as money and jewelry. Indians living on the East Coast used to catch marginellas by baiting their fishing lines with oysters. When the oysters became covered with these tiny snails, the line was pulled up very slowly and the shells picked off.

Carmine Marginella
Color this shell brownish rose. It is 1/3 in. high, found from southern Florida to the Caribbean. (103)

Tan Marginella
This shell is a rich golden tan. Also 1/3 in. high, it is found from North Carolina to the Caribbean. (104)

Orange Marginella
A bright honey orange shell, 3/4 in. high. Found from southern Florida to the West Indies. (105)

Princess Marginella
Color this marginella tan, with reddish brown bands. The white marks are outlined with shades of brown. Shell 1/2 in. high; found from the Florida Keys to the West Indies. (106)

Orange-banded Marginella
Color the outside of this shell creamy white, with three orange bands. The inside is orangish brown. Shell 1/2 in. high; found from North Carolina to the Caribbean. (107)

Olive Shells

Olive shells are small, but the animals that live in them are relatively large. The snail's mantle and foot, when extended, may completely cover the shell. This keeps the shell smooth and glossy. Olive snails are scavengers that eat crabs and clams. They are found on both coasts of the United States, on sandy beaches.

Purple Dwarf Olive
The outside of this shell is purplish or brownish gray. It has an orange band over dark lines at the top. A violet band runs along the seam line near the bottom. The inside is purple. Shell ½ to 1½ in. high; found from British Columbia to Baja California. (108)

West Indian Dwarf Olive
A yellowish white shell with brownish rose markings in bands. Shell ½ to 1¼ in. high; found from Florida to Texas and south to the West Indies. (109)

Jasper Dwarf Olive
Color this shell cream, with pinkish brown lines and spots. It is ½ to ⅞ in. high, and is found from southeastern Florida to Venezuela. (110)

Netted Olive
A creamy white shell with reddish brown, netlike lines. It is 1⅛ to 2¼ in. high, and found from southeastern Florida to Venezuela. (111)

Lettered Olive
Color the outside grayish yellow, with reddish brown, zigzag markings. Shell 1¾ to 2¾ in. high; found from North Carolina to Texas and south to Brazil. (112)

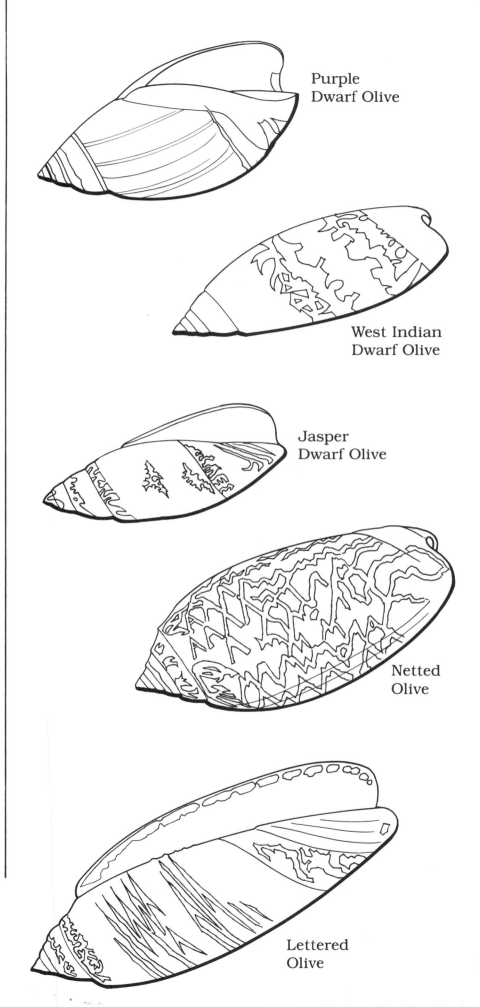

Purple Dwarf Olive

West Indian Dwarf Olive

Jasper Dwarf Olive

Netted Olive

Lettered Olive

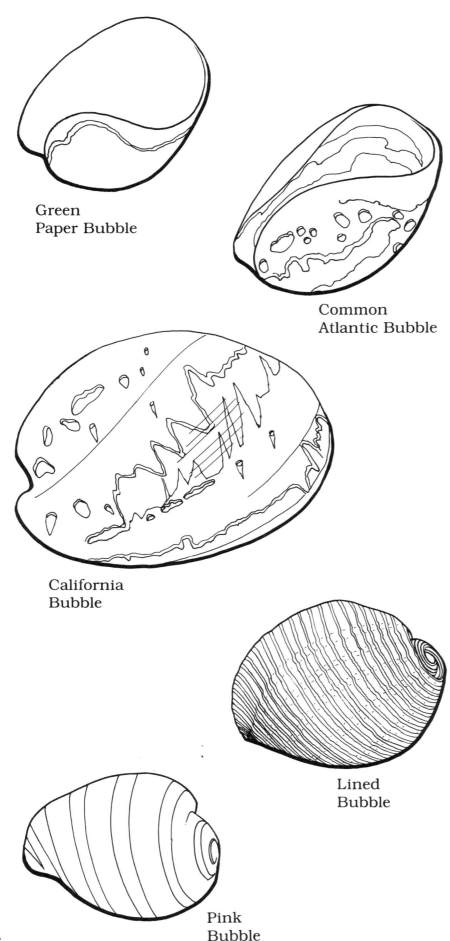

Green
Paper Bubble

Common
Atlantic Bubble

California
Bubble

Lined
Bubble

Pink
Bubble

Bubble Shells

Bubble shells are often smaller than the animals that live in them. The shells are thin and fragile. The snails each have two pairs of feelers, and are hermaphroditic — each one has both male and female sex organs. Bubble snails are found in shallow water, in warm and tropical seas.

Green Paper Bubble
This bubble shell is yellowish green both inside and out. Shell ½ to ¾ in. high; found from Puget Sound to the Gulf of California. (113)

Common Atlantic Bubble
A whitish shell mottled with pink and reddish brown. It has tan spots and streaks. Shell ½ to 1⅛ in. high; found from Florida to Brazil. (114)

California Bubble
This shell is sometimes called Gould's Bubble. It is mottled grayish brown, with dark brown streaks lined with white on one side. Shell 1½ to 2½ in. high; found from southern California to the Gulf of California. (115)

Lined Bubble
A white shell with dark brown and orange lines. It is ¾ to 1¾ in. high; found from southern Florida to Brazil. (116)

Pink Bubble
Color this shell pink, with bands of brown and white. A 1-in. shell, found on Hawaiian shores. (117)

True Limpet Shells

The conical shell of a true lim-pet is shaped like a Chinese hat. Unlike the shells of key-hole limpets (next page), these shells have no holes in the top and are open only at the base. The snails have a foot, two feelers, and a mouth. Those that live on rocks in cool, deep water have a higher shell than those that live on seaweed. They feed on plants at night, and are found on rocks below the low-tide line. Limpets can be eaten raw or cooked. Some of the shells are used as jew-elry.

White-cap Limpet
Color this shell pinkish white. It is ¾ to 1¾ in. long, found from Alaska to Baja California. (118)

Atlantic Plate Limpet
A pale bluish gray and tan shell, with reddish brown streaks. Shell ⅞ to 1¾ in. long; found on both coasts. (119)

Giant Owl Limpet
This shell got its name from an owl-shaped scar on its inside. The inside of the shell is light blue, with a wide brown mar-gin. Shell 1⅓ to 4¼ in. long; found from Washington to Baja California. (120)

Rough Limpet
Color this limpet shell greenish gray and black. Shell ¾ to 2 in. long; found from Alaska to Mex-ico. (121)

White-cap
Limpet

Atlantic
Plate Limpet

Giant Owl
Limpet

Rough
Limpet

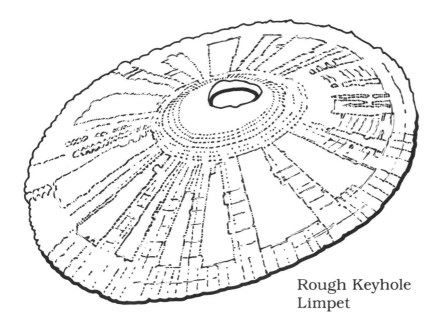

Rough Keyhole
Limpet

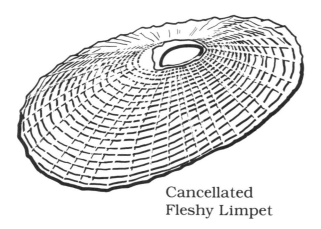

Cancellated
Fleshy Limpet

Linné's
Puncturella

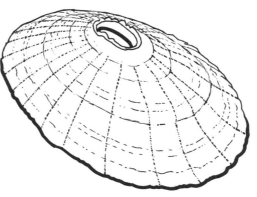

Volcano
Limpet

Keyhole Limpet Shells

These volcano-shaped shells generally have a hole, slit, or groove near the top, but some species have a slit at the margin near the hind end. Water enters the shell through the bottom and washes over the snail's gills, providing the animal with oxygen. The water then goes out the "keyhole" in the top, carrying away the snail's waste. Most keyhole limpets are plant-eaters that feed on algae-covered rocks during the night. They are found on rocks at the low-tide line.

Rough Keyhole Limpet
Color this shell light gray, with purple-brown rays. It is 1 to 2¾ in. long, and is found from Alaska to Baja California. (122)

Cancellated Fleshy Limpet
A pale purple shell, tinged with gray. It has pinkish brown rays. Shell ⅝ to 1½ in. long; found from Florida to Brazil. (123)

Linné's Puncturella
This keyhole limpet shell is white and gray-brown. It is ¼ to ½ in. long, and is found from Alaska to Baja California. (124)

Volcano Limpet
Color this shell greenish, with red around the "keyhole." Dark red streaks run down the sides, making the shell look like an erupting volcano. Shell 1 to 1⅝ in. long; found from the Florida Keys to the West Indies. (125)

Abalone Shells

The largest and most beautiful of all Pacific Coast shells. Most abalones are good to eat. Most live in shallow water on rocks, but some can be found in water as deep as 1,200 ft. The holes in the side of the shell let water out after it has passed over the snail's gills, supplying the animal with oxygen. Abalones feed on algae and giant kelp; in turn, they are fed on by man and the sea otter. The decorative shells have been used for such things as jewelry.

The collecting of abalones is strictly controlled.

Red Abalone
Color the outside of this shell light red to reddish brown. Color the inside pink, pale blue, yellow-green, and gray-green, with an orange rim. Shell up to 12 in. long; found in water 20 to 40 ft. deep, from Oregon to Baja California. (126)

Green Abalone
The outside of this abalone shell is olive and reddish brown. The inside has iridescent shades of blue and green. Shell 6 to 8 in. long; found in water 10 to 25 ft. deep, from Oregon to Baja California. (127)

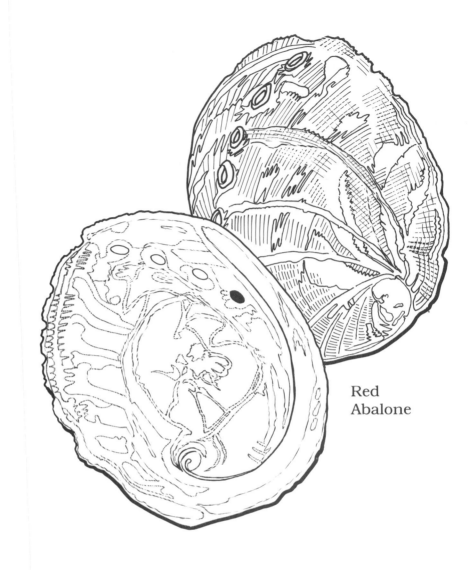

Red
Abalone

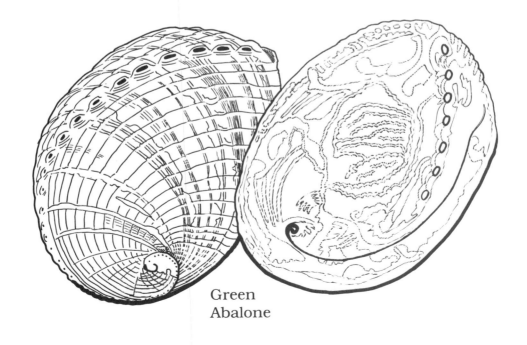

Green
Abalone

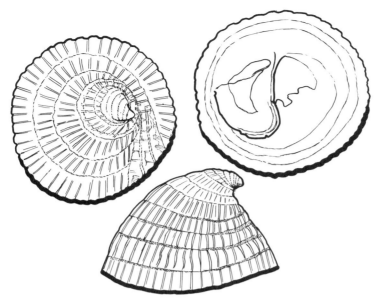

Striate
Cup-and-saucer Shell

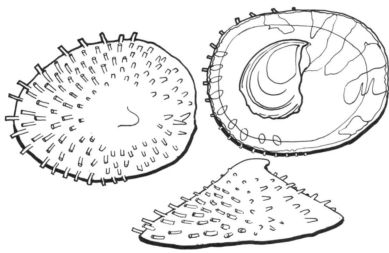

Spiny
Cup-and-saucer Shell

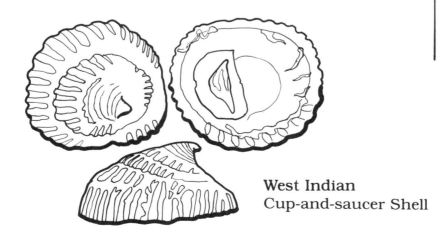

West Indian
Cup-and-saucer Shell

Cup-and-saucer Shells

Cup-and-saucer shells have a little cup inside that supports the animal's body. The young can move about freely, but after two years they attach themselves to a rock or shell and remain there all their life. These limpets strain algae from the water that passes through their gills. The snails are hermaphroditic — each animal is both male and female. They are found world-wide in both warm and cold waters.

Striate Cup-and-saucer Shell
The outside of this shell is yellow and pinkish gray. Color the inside orange, with a white and yellow cup. Shell ½ to 1⅜ in. wide; found in moderate to deep water, from southern Canada to Florida. (128)

Spiny Cup-and-saucer Shell
A light yellow shell, mottled with reddish brown. The inside is mottled with reddish brown and orangish brown on light yellow. The cup is white. Shell ¾ to 2 in. wide; found on rocks or dead shells, in water from a few to 180 ft. deep from California to Chile. (129)

West Indian Cup-and-saucer Shell
This shell is also called the Rosy Cup-and-saucer Shell. The outside is gray and white. Color the inside pinkish, with light orange accents. The cup is white and orange. Shell ¾ to 1 in. wide; found in shallow water from southern Florida to the West Indies. (130)

Slipper Shells

These "boat shells" have a little shelf that makes them look like an old sailing ship with a deck. This shelf supports the living animal. Like cup-and-saucer snails, these mollusks settle down after two years of drifting and remain attached to a rock or dead shell for the rest of their lives. They strain algae-laden water through their gills, and are hermaphroditic. Slipper shells are found in shallow water all over the world.

Spiny Slipper Shell
The outside of this shell is white to orange-brown. The inside is a mottled yellow-brown with a white shelf. Shell ½ to 1¼ in. long; found on both coasts of the United States, in all southeastern states to the West Indies, and from California to Chile. (131)

Spotted Slipper Shell
This shell is cream with chocolate brown spots inside and out. The shelf is white. Shell ½ to 1½ in. long; found in western Florida. (132)

Atlantic Slipper Shell
A buff-colored shell, with pinkish or reddish brown marks. The inside is white, marked with purple-brown and orange. The shelf is white. Shell ¾ to 2½ in. long; found from Canada to Florida and on the West Coast. It also occurs in parts of Europe. (133)

Convex Slipper Shell
Color the outside golden yellow-brown. The inside is reddish brown, with a whitish shelf. Shell ⅜ to ¾ in. long; found from Massachusetts to the West Indies, and also along the Pacific Coast. (134)

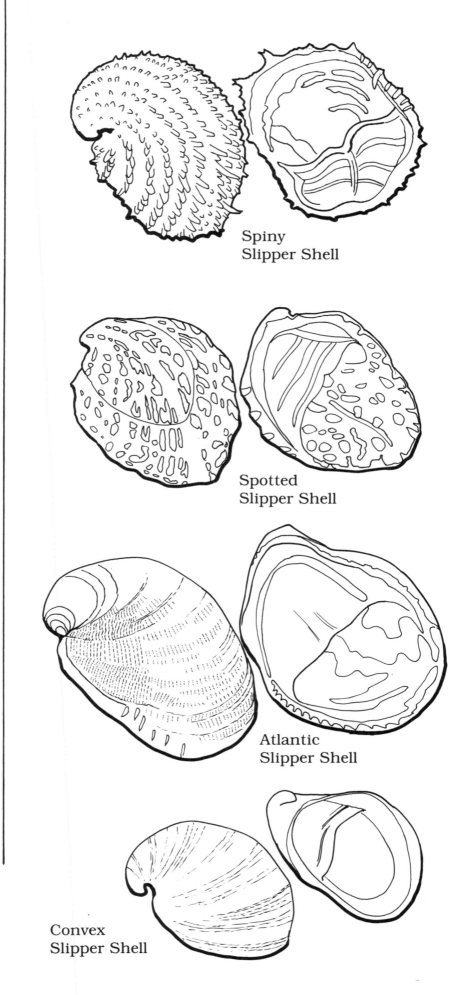

Spiny
Slipper Shell

Spotted
Slipper Shell

Atlantic
Slipper Shell

Convex
Slipper Shell

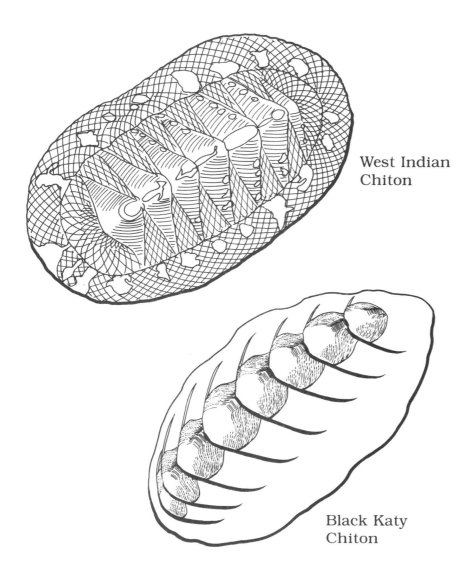

West Indian
Chiton

Black Katy
Chiton

Red Northern
Chiton

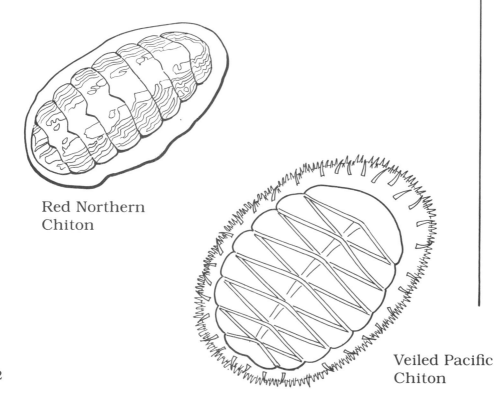

Veiled Pacific
Chiton

Chiton Shells

One of the seven classes of mollusks, chitons (pronounced kyé-ton) have been around for about 570 million years. The most primitive of mollusks, chitons have a shell made up of eight plates held together with a tough leathery skin, or girdle. These plates overlap like medieval armor or a "coat of mail," which is a nickname for these shells. All chiton shells are symmetrical and oval. Most species live under rocks, stones, and dead shells, feeding at night on algae or particles of animal and plant life. These shells are found on both coasts in the zones where the water is warm, but mostly on the Pacific Coast.

West Indian Chiton
This chiton shell is light and dark shades of greenish gray and brown. A common shell, 1¼ to 3¼ in. long. It is found in the intertidal zone from southeastern Florida to the West Indies. (135)

Black Katy Chiton
Color this shell black, with light and dark tan plates. Shell 1½ to 3 in. long; found below the low-tide line, from Alaska to California. (136)

Red Northern Chiton
A pale orange shell, mottled with darker orange and red. Shell ½ to 1 in. long; found just below the low-tide line, in water 450 ft. deep on both coasts. (137)

Veiled Pacific Chiton
Color the girdle, or outside edge, reddish yellow. The plates are olive brown, with tan, pink, blue, and red-brown streaks. Shell 1 to 2 in. long; found in the intertidal zone in California. (138)

Scallop Shells

Scallops are a large, free-swimming family of mollusks found worldwide. They have a row of tentacles and tiny, well-developed eyes along the outer edge of the mantle (the membrane lining the shell). Adult scallops propel themselves by rapidly opening and closing their two shells with a large muscle, forcing out a jet of water. This muscle is the part we eat; many species are edible. Artists have long been inspired by the simple, elegant shape of these shells.

Giant Pacific Scallop
A pinkish gray and buff shell, home to an edible scallop. Shell 6 to 11 in. high; found in deep water from Alaska to California. (139)

Pacific Pink Scallop
Color this shell pink, with paler pink rays and darker pink semicircles. Shell 2 to 3¼ in. high; found in shallow water from Alaska to California. (140)

Atlantic Deep-sea Scallop
This scallop shell has light and dark, dusty rose rays. The scallop is edible. Shell 2 to 8 in. high; found in deep water from Canada to North Carolina. (141)

Lion's Paw
A collector's favorite. This red shell is 2½ to 6 in. long. It is found in deep water, from North Carolina to Brazil. (142)

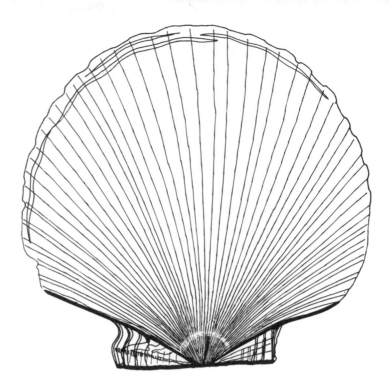

Giant Pacific
Scallop

Pacific Pink
Scallop

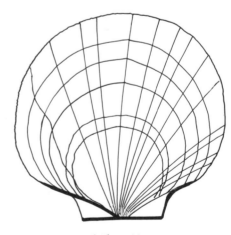

Atlantic
Deep-sea
Scallop

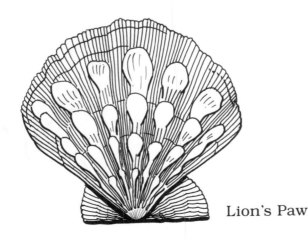

Lion's Paw

43

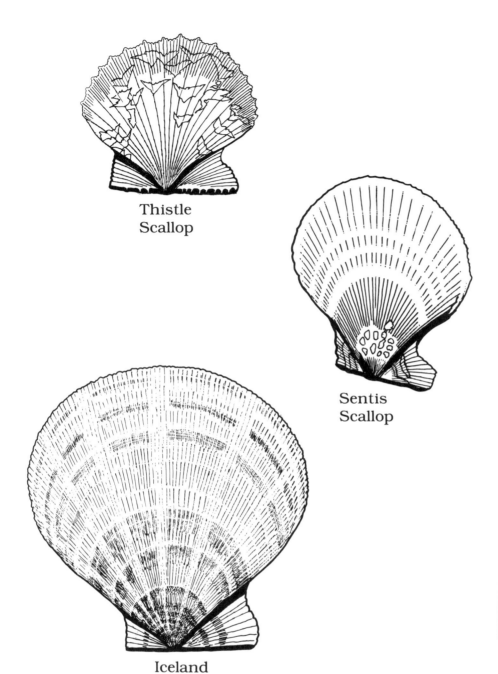

Thistle
Scallop

Sentis
Scallop

Iceland
Scallop

Thistle Scallop
A rough, thorny shell. Color it bright red, with white patches. Shell ½ to 1½ in. high; found in water 10 to 150 ft. deep, from South Carolina to South America. (143)

Sentis Scallop
Color this thorny shell light and dark purple. It is 1 to 1⅝ in. high, and is found in water 1 to 500 ft. deep from North Carolina to southeastern Florida and the West Indies. (144)

Iceland Scallop
This shell is yellow, with light gray rays and darker yellow semicircles. It houses an edible scallop. Shell 1¾ to 4 in. high; found in water 6 to 1,000 ft. deep, from the Arctic to Massachusetts and from Alaska to Washington. (145)

Calico Scallop
Color this shell pink, with yellow rays and red-brown flecks. Shell 1 to 2¾ in. high; found in water 5 to 300 ft. deep, from North Carolina to southern Florida. (146)

Hinds' Scallop
A lavender scallop shell with dark peach semicircles. Shell 1 to 2½ in. high; found in water 1 to 600 ft. deep from Alaska to California. (147)

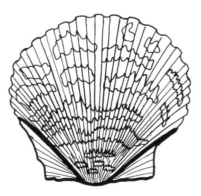

Calico
Scallop

Hinds'
Scallop

Ark Shells

Most ark shells are found in tropical and temperate seas, and are more common along the Atlantic than the Pacific coast. The sturdy shell is oblong in shape, and most species have a prominent projection called an "ear." Ark shells are heavily ribbed, with many small teeth on the hinge. Some species burrow in mud or sand, while others nestle between rocks, anchoring themselves with hairlike threads. The animals are used for bait and food in the Caribbean.

Eared Ark
Color this shell grayish white. Shell 1½ to 3½ in. long; found in mud or sand, in shallow water from North Carolina to Brazil. (148)

Turkey Wing
A yellowish white ark shell, with reddish brown stripes. Shell 1¾ to 3½ in. long; found between rocks, in shallow to deep water from North Carolina to Brazil. (149)

Blood Ark
This is one of the few cold-water arks. It is also one of the very few mollusks that has hemoglobin in its blood, which makes it red. Color the shell yellowish or grayish white. The growth rings are grayish. Shell 1⅛ to 3 in. long; found in mud or sand, in shallow to deep water from Massachusetts to Brazil. (150)

Baily's Miniature Ark
Color this ark shell yellowish to brownish white. Shell ¼ to ⅜ in. long; found under rocks at the low-tide line, from lower California to the Gulf of California. (151)

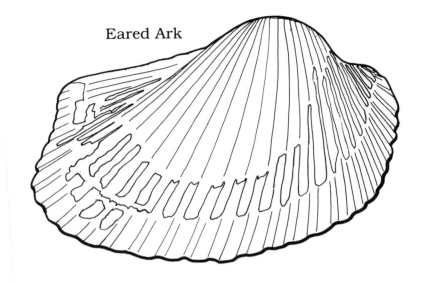
Eared Ark

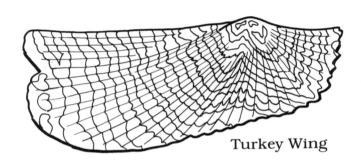
Turkey Wing

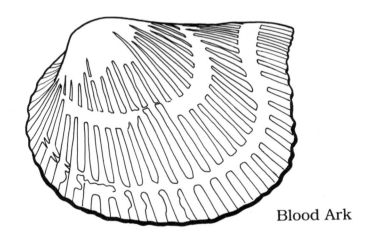
Blood Ark

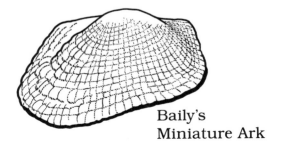
Baily's
Miniature Ark

45

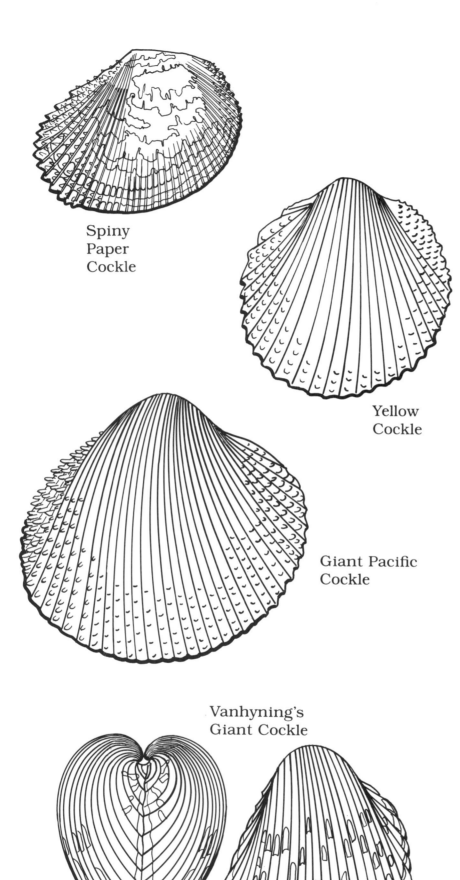

Spiny
Paper
Cockle

Yellow
Cockle

Giant Pacific
Cockle

Vanhyning's
Giant Cockle

Cockle Shells

Cockle shells are found world-wide in all seas. They are also known as "heart shells" because of their shape. They may be ribbed, smooth, prickly, fat, or thin, but all are heart-shaped when viewed from the end. They have strong hinge teeth. A short, fringed inhale siphon brings in food and water, while an exhale siphon takes out waste. The long, usually brightly colored foot enables the cockle to burrow, or to jump several inches off the sea bottom. Many American species are eaten by both fishes and man. Street vendors once drew customers by calling "Cockles and mussels, alive-alive-O."

Spiny Paper Cockle
Color this fairly fragile shell off-white, with lilac rose markings. A moderately common shell, 1 to 1¾ in. high; found in moderately shallow water from North Carolina to the West Indies. (152)

Yellow Cockle
This thick shell is very common. Color it cream to yellow, with reddish orange patches. Shell 1¼ to 2¼ in. high; found in shallow water from North Carolina to the West Indies. (153)

Giant Pacific Cockle
Color this large, oval, spiny shell a creamy tan, with orangish to orange-tan markings. Shell 3 to 6 in. high; found in mud or sand, from the shore to deep water in central and southern California. (154)

Vanhyning's Giant Cockle
A common shell, glossy and vividly colored. Make it a pale straw color, with reddish brown to rusty orange spots on the ribs. The edge is purple-brown. Shell 3½ to 5 in. high; found in mud or sand, from shallow to deep water in southwestern Florida. (155)

Lucine Shells

These are solid, circular shells. A long, narrow muscle scar toward the front on the inside shows where the animal was attached. The mollusk uses its long, wormlike foot to make a mucus-lined hole in the sand. This hole serves as an inhale tube through which the animal draws water and food. A very long exhale siphon can be pulled up inside the shell, much like a glove with the fingers turned inside-out. Almost all lucines lie buried in mud or sand, in shallow to deep water worldwide.

Tiger Lucine
Color the inside of this lucine shell light to darker yellow, shading to an orangish rose on the edges. The outside is white, with a rose tinge near the hinge. Shell 2 to 3¾ in. long; found from southern Florida to Brazil. (156)

Buttercup Lucine
The inside of this shell is golden yellow to orange, with a white edge. Color the outside grayish white, tinged with pinkish yellow. Shell 1¼ to 2½ in. long; found from North Carolina to the Caribbean. (157)

Cross-hatched Lucine
This shell is white, both inside and out. Shell ⅜ to 1 in. high; found from Massachusetts to Brazil. (158)

Lovely Miniature Lucine
Color the outside grayish white. The inside is white. Shell ¼ to ⅜ in. long; found from Virginia to the Bahamas and the Gulf of Mexico. (159)

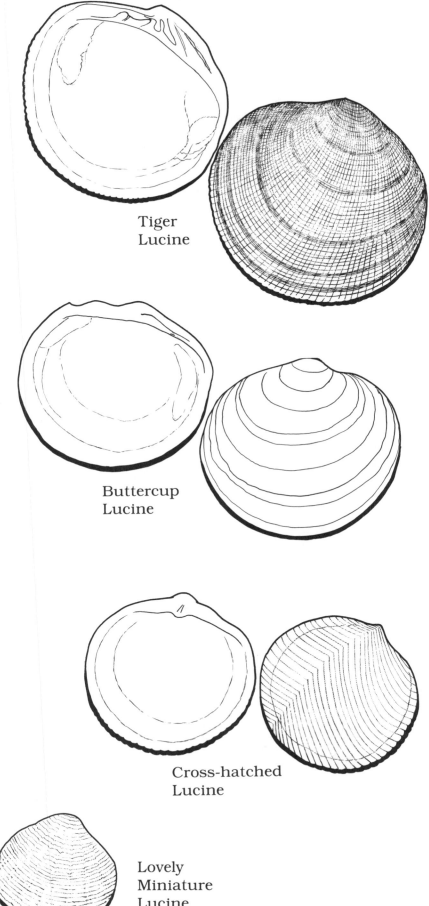

Tiger
Lucine

Buttercup
Lucine

Cross-hatched
Lucine

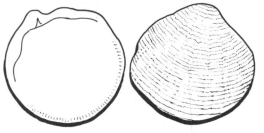

Lovely
Miniature
Lucine

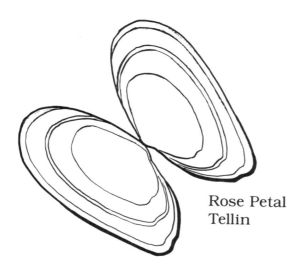

Rose Petal
Tellin

Tellin Shells

A large family, found world-wide in shallow to deep water. Tellin shells have a slight twist to the right at the hind end, plus two main teeth on the hinge. Most are smooth and shiny, with varying bright colors. Tellins avoid enemies by using their large foot to hastily dig a burrow or to move upwards or sideways. They live in mud, sand, or gravel, and eat rotting plant material. They have two siphons: a long tube that brings in food particles, and a short tube that takes out water and waste.

Rose Petal Tellin
Color this tellin shell light to dark cherry pink. It is ⅝ to 1½ in. long, found from northern Florida to Brazil. (160)

Sunrise Tellin
A white shell with pink and yellow rays. Shell 2 to 4 in. long; found from South Carolina to South America. (161)

Salmon Tellin
A whitish shell, stained with salmon pink and marked with brown growth lines. Shell ½ to ¾ in. long; found from Alaska to California. (162)

Candy Stick Tellin
This semi-transparent shell is yellowish white, with candy pink rays. Shell ⅝ to 1⅛ in. long; found from North Carolina to Brazil. (163)

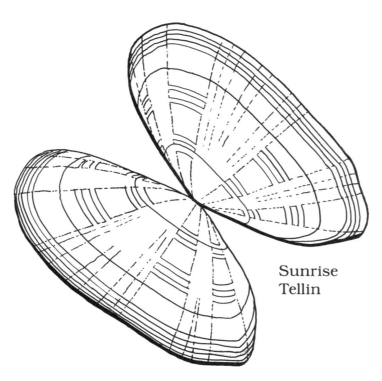

Sunrise
Tellin

Salmon
Tellin

Candy Stick
Tellin

48

Donax Shells

A small family of often brightly colored, wedge-shaped little clams. They lie buried in moist sand, keeping their two siphons just above the surface. If a wave washes them out of the sand, they quickly dig back in with their large foot. Their shell is thick and triangular, with two main teeth plus a smaller tooth in the front and another in the rear. These "bean" or "butterfly" clams are found close to shore in nearly all tropical seas, and also along coastlines that are not heavily polluted. They make a delicious clam broth.

Coquina
This shell varies in color; individuals may be white to yellow, orange, pink, red-purple, blue, and deep purple. Rays or bands are often present, and sometimes a shell has both. Shell ½ to 1 in. long; found from New York to Mexico. (164)

Gould's Donax
Another variable shell. Color these three specimens yellowish white or bluish, sometimes with rosy or light purple rays. Shell ⅝ to ⅞ in. long; found from South Carolina to Mexico. (165)

California Donax
Color these donax shells yellowish white. Shell ½ to 1 in. long; found from California to Mexico. (166)

Fat Gulf Donax
Whitish shells, with a purplish tinge. Shell ½ in. long; found from northwestern Florida to Texas. (167)

Fossor Donax
Color these two examples bluish or creamy white, with light purple rays. Shell ½ in. long; found from New York to New Jersey. (168)

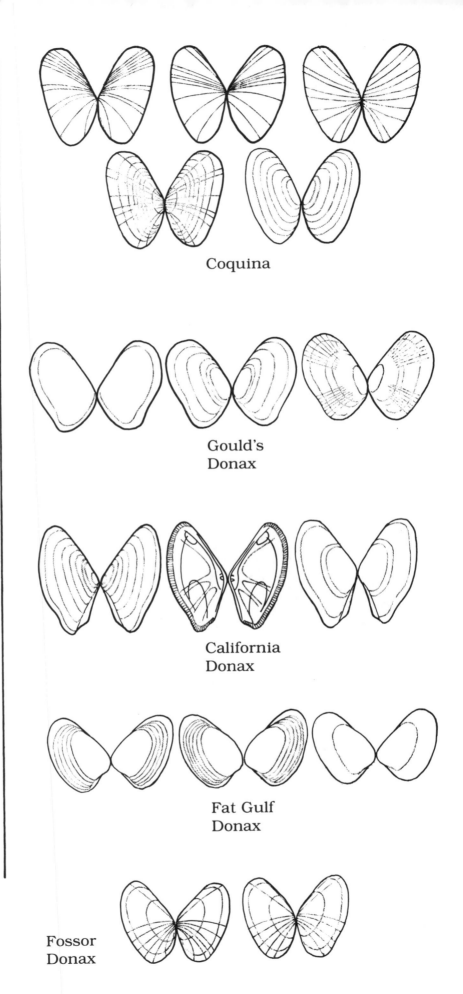

Coquina

Gould's
Donax

California
Donax

Fat Gulf
Donax

Fossor
Donax

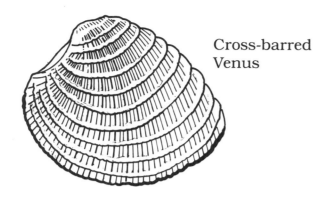

Cross-barred
Venus

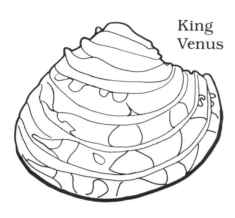

King
Venus

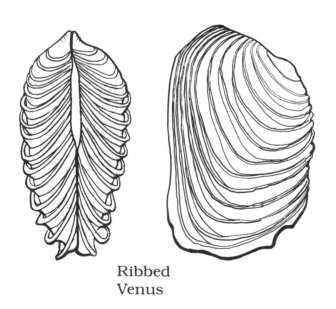

Ribbed
Venus

Venus Clam Shells

A very large family of thick-shelled clams, found in all seas. Both of their shells are the same size and shape, and the hinges have interlocking teeth. Each animal has two separate siphons for circulating water. A large, hatchet-shaped foot allows them to move about freely, and to burrow just under the surface of mud or sand. Clams have been used for food since prehistoric times.

Cross-barred Venus
Color this shell buffy white, with brown rays and marks. Shell 1¾ in. long; found from North Carolina to Brazil. (169)

King Venus
Color this shiny shell grayish white, marked with lilac and brown. Shell 1½ to 2 in. long; found from southern Florida to the West Indies. (170)

Ribbed Venus
An unusual-looking clam shell. It is white. Shell 1½ in. long; found in California. (171)

Elegant Venus
This shell is also called the Royal Comb Shell. Color it light lavender, with purple marks. An uncommon shell, 2 in. long; found from Texas to the Caribbean. (172)

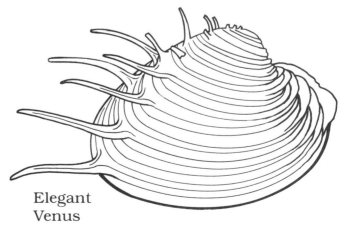

Elegant
Venus

Northern Quahog

This clam is the most important edible bivalve sold along the East Coast. It has many names: cherrystone, little neck, round clam, hard-shelled clam. The Algonquin Indians of New England called it *quahog*. It is the shell Indian money, or "wampum," was made from. Color the outside gray to yellow, with a buffy tinge. The inside is white, with a purple spot near the hind end. Shell 2¾ to 4½ in. long; found from Canada to Florida. (173)

Pismo Clam

This clam is an important, delicious food in California. Commercial digging is not allowed, and private diggers are limited to 15 clams per day, per person. The shell is smooth and polished. Color it brownish cream, with purplish brown rays. Shell 2½ to 6¼ in. long; found from California to Mexico. (174)

Pointed Venus

Color this shell a light blue-gray, marked with tan and darker blue-gray lines. Shell ½ to 1 in. long; found from southern Florida to Texas and south to Mexico. (175)

Lightning Venus

A white shell with brown marks. Shell 1 to 2 in. long; found from North Carolina to Brazil. (176)

Glory-of-the-seas Venus

This shell is white, with red-brown shadings. A rare shell, 1 in. long; found from North Carolina to Texas in deep water. (177)

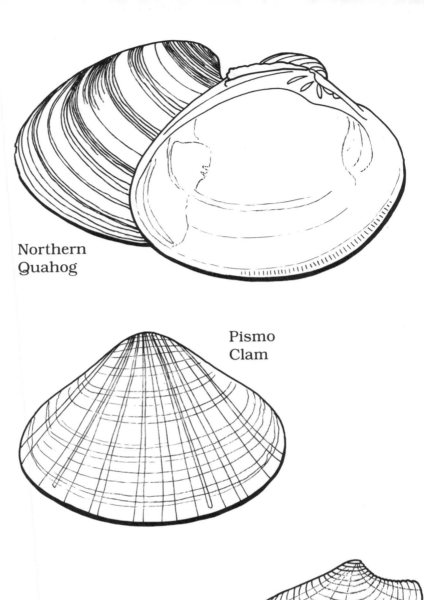

Northern Quahog

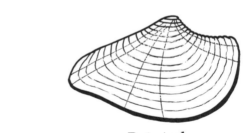

Pismo Clam

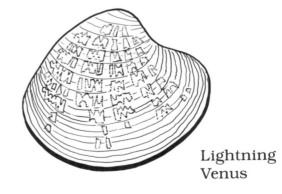

Pointed Venus

Lightning Venus

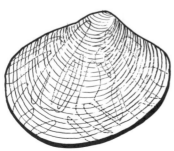

Glory-of-the-seas Venus

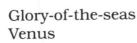

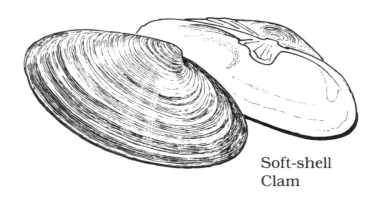

Soft-shell
Clam

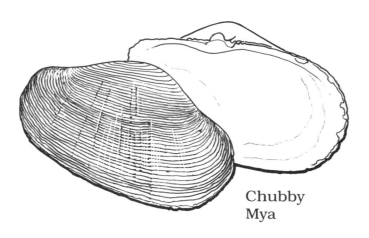

Chubby
Mya

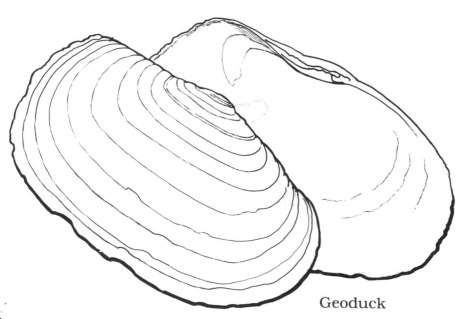

Geoduck

Gaper Clam Shells

A small family of soft-shelled clams, found in cool water in all seas. Their chalk-white, thin shells are mostly oblong in shape, open at both ends or the hind end, and cannot close completely. The hinge is on the left valve. A thin skin, or periostracum, covers the outside of the shell. This skin dries up and can flake off when the shell is out of water. The clam has a retractable siphon covered by a long tube. Gaper clams burrow in mud, muddy sand, or clay. You can find them at low tide by watching for the little squirts of water from their siphons above the sand.

Soft-shell Clam
A delicious clam with many names: steamer, gaper, manninose. Color the outside of the shell blue-gray to grayish white. The inside is white. Shell 1 to 5½ in. long; found from Arctic seas to North Carolina, and from British Columbia to central California. (178)

Chubby Mya
This shell's periostracum is pale yellow to rusty brown. The shell itself is white. Shell 1¾ to 3 in. long; found from British Columbia to lower California. (179)

Geoduck
The American Indians called this mollusk *gweduck* ("gooey-duck"). The thick-shelled clam cannot retract its siphon. A yellow-brown periostracum covers this grayish white shell. The inside is white. Shell 3½ to 9 in. long; found from southern Alaska to Baja California. One of the best clams to eat. (180)

Sanguin Clam Shells

Rounded, oval bivalves, with one shell flatter than the other. The shells have small hinge teeth and are slightly open at one end, to accommodate the clam's long siphons. A strong ligament controls the opening and closing of the shells. Sanguin clams are found chiefly in warm seas. They are rapid burrowers and live in mud, gravel, or sandy mud.

Atlantic Sanguinolaria
A rosy pink shell, blending to whitish on the edges. Shell 1½ to 2 in. long; found from southern Florida and the Gulf States to the West Indies. (181)

Nuttall's Mahogany Clam
The periostracum, or tough skin, of this clam shell is a shiny nut brown. The shell underneath is bluish white, with purple rays. Shell 2½ to 3¾ in. long; found from southern California to Baja California. (182)

Gaudy Asaphis
This shell's colors are variable; it may be yellow, orange, blue, or purple. The glossy inside colors also vary. Shell 1½ to 2½ in. long; found from southeastern Florida to the West Indies. (183)

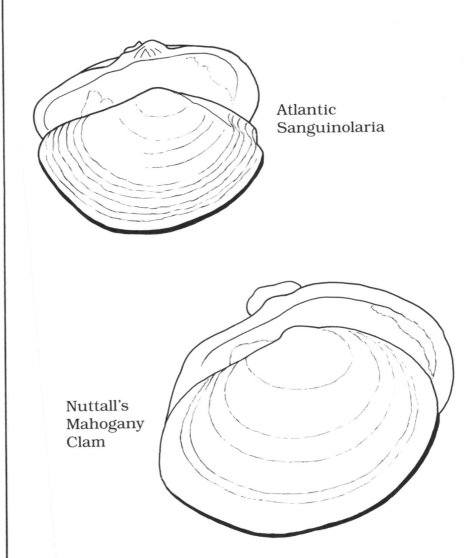

Atlantic Sanguinolaria

Nuttall's Mahogany Clam

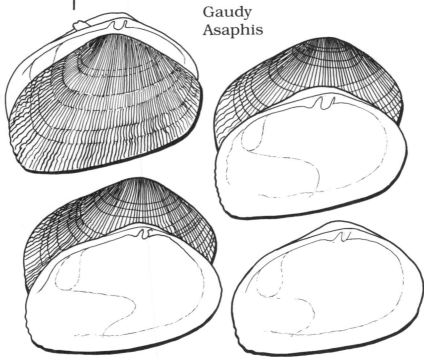

Gaudy Asaphis

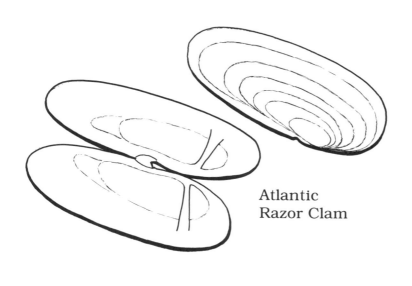

Atlantic
Razor Clam

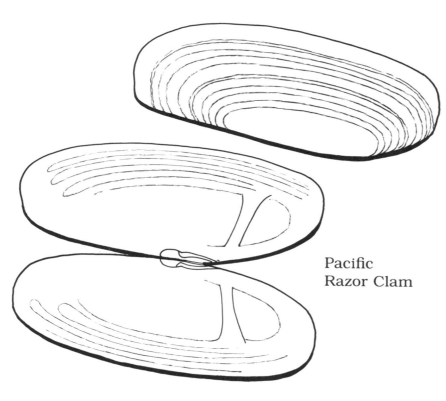

Pacific
Razor Clam

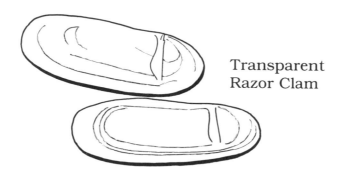

Transparent
Razor Clam

Razor Clam Shells

These elongate, oval shells are strengthened by a straight, raised rib on the inside. The hinge is off-center toward the front, and the shell is agape at each end. Except for growth lines, the shell is smooth. Razor clam shells have a periostracum. The clam's long, curved, powerful foot allows it to burrow rapidly and move easily along the bottom. It folds its foot back tightly against the shell like a wound spring and then suddenly lets it go, propelling itself forward 3 or 4 ft. When this process is rapidly repeated, the mollusk zigzags quickly out of sight. Razor clams are found in mud or sand, in a vertical position with about 2 in. of the razor-sharp shell sticking out. They live worldwide and are delicious to eat. Some are sold commercially.

Atlantic Razor Clam
Color the outside of this shell iridescent purple, with an olive-brown periostracum at the edges. The inside is purplish white. Shell 1½ to 2⅝ in. long; found from Canada to North Carolina. (184)

Pacific Razor Clam
This shell has a tough, olive-brown periostracum. The inside is white, washed with purple. Shell 3 to 6¼ in. long; found from Alaska to California. (185)

Transparent Razor Clam
A transparent white shell with a rosy purple tinge near the front end and splotches on the hind end. Shell 1 to 1½ in. long; found from central California to Baja California. (186)

Piddock Shells

Delicate, winglike shells, widely agape at both ends. The animals that live in these brittle white shells have siphons that are sometimes more than twice as long as their bodies. Some species can retract their siphons; others cannot. All have a strong foot with a suction plate on the end. One end of their shell is very rough, and by turning and twisting they bore holes, flushing away debris with jets of water. Some piddock shells burrow as deep as two feet in stiff mud, clay, peat, or soft rock. Others bore into hard rock, coral, wood, lead, and plastic, and are very destructive. They are found in all seas.

Angel Wing
Some rare Angel Wings have a pinkish tinge, but these shells are usually all white. The meat is good to eat. Shell 4 to 8 in. long; found from Massachusetts to Brazil. (187)

Campeche Angel Wing
This uncommon shell is white to grayish white. Shell 2 to 4¾ in. long; found from North Carolina to Brazil. (188)

Fallen Angel Wing
A white to grayish white shell, 1¼ to 2¾ in. long. Found from Maine to Brazil. (189)

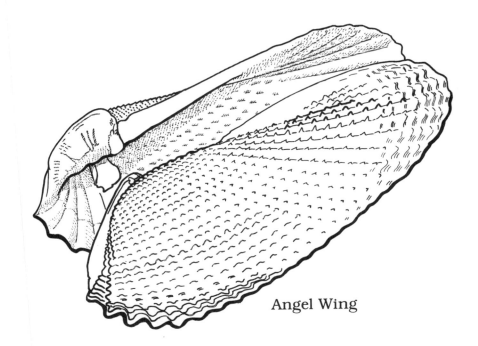

Angel Wing

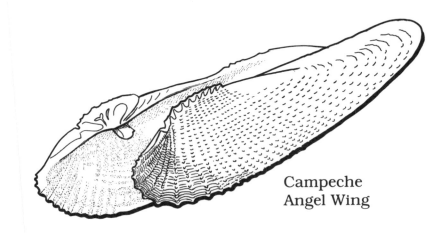

Campeche Angel Wing

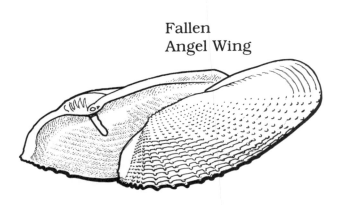

Fallen Angel Wing

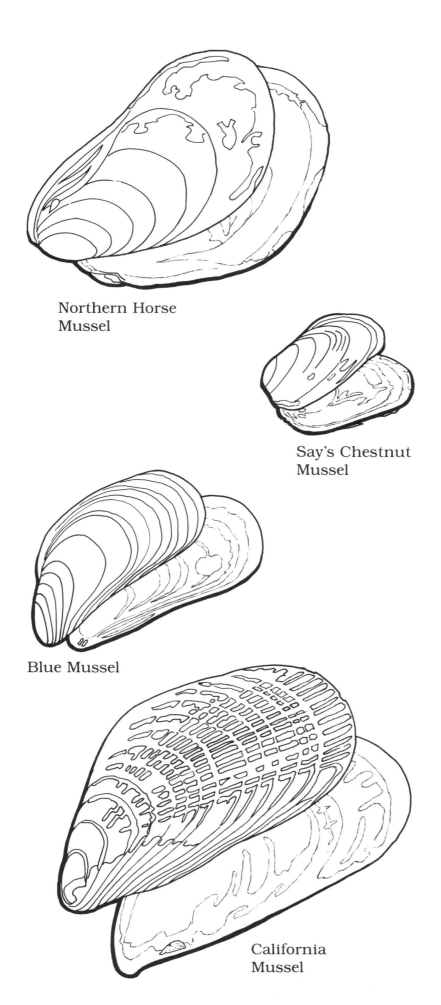

Northern Horse
Mussel

Say's Chestnut
Mussel

Blue Mussel

California
Mussel

Mussel Shells

A large family of bivalves, with a pair of equal-sized shells. The shell's hinge has no teeth, and the inside is iridescent. A tough skin, the periostracum, covers the shell. Mussels live in dense colonies throughout the world, mostly in cool water. All mussels anchor themselves to rocks, wood, or other surfaces with a byssus—a series of tough, sticky, hairlike threads that harden into an anchor. Mussels move by breaking their threads and using their foot. They spin a new byssus after finding a suitable place to anchor. Many mussels are delicious to eat, but when they feed on toxic algae they can become poisonous.

Northern Horse Mussel
A bit of pale, iridescent gray shell shows through the brown periostracum. The inside is gray and white. Shell 2 to 9 in. long; found among gravel or rocks from the Arctic to New Jersey and in California. (190)

Say's Chestnut Mussel
The periostracum on this mussel shell is light to dark brown. The shell itself is bluish gray. The inside is a rosy purplish gray. Shell ¾ to 1½ in. long; found in sand or mud from South Carolina to the West Indies. (191)

Blue Mussel
The outside of this iridescent shell is purple-gray. The inside is bluish white, with a bluish purple edge. Shell 1¼ to 4 in. long; found from the Arctic to South Carolina and in California. (192)

California Mussel
Patches of purplish tan shell show through the dark brown periostracum. Color the inside iridescent grayish to tan. Shell 2 to 10 in. long; found on rocks from Alaska to Mexico. (193)

Scorched Mussel
Color the outside light brownish gray. The inside is purplish, with red-purple splotches. Shell ⅝ to 1⅝ in. long; found on rocks and pilings from North Carolina to Brazil. (194)

Tulip Mussel
This iridescent shell is light pinkish purple to rosy red. Color the inside a pearly purple-gray, with red showing through. Shell 1¼ to 4 in. long; found on moss-covered rocks from South Carolina to Brazil. (195)

Hooked Mussel
This shell is purple with light blue ribs. Inside, it is purple to pinkish purple, with a light blue edge. Shell 1 to 2⅜ in. long; found on oyster beds and pilings from Maryland to the West Indies. (196)

Yellow Mussel
Color the thin outer skin bright yellow. The inside is pearly yellowish gray, mottled with red or purple-brown. Shell ⅞ to 1⅝ in. long; found on rocks from southern Florida to the West Indies. (197)

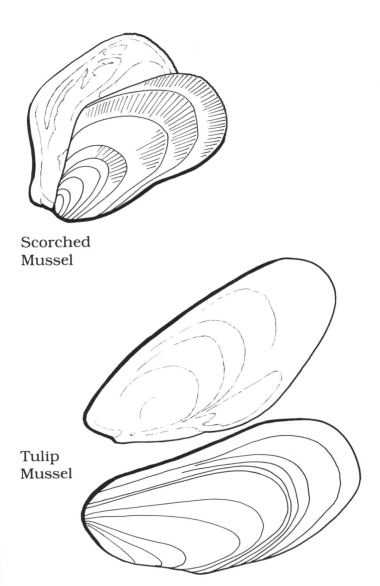

Scorched
Mussel

Tulip
Mussel

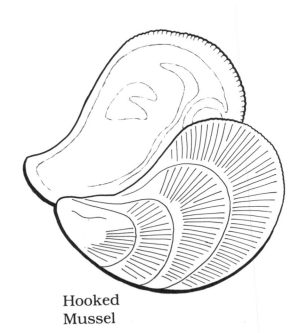

Hooked
Mussel

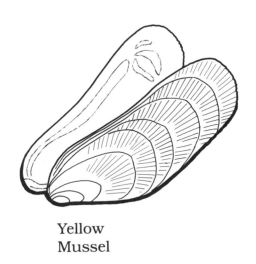

Yellow
Mussel

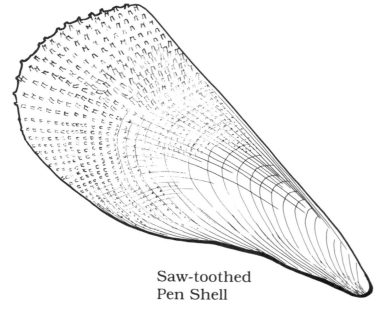

Saw-toothed
Pen Shell

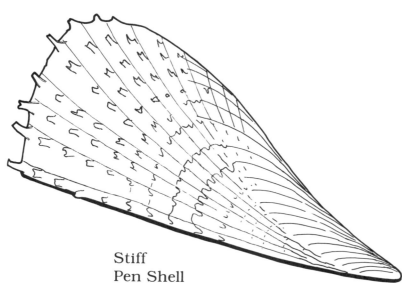

Stiff
Pen Shell

Pen Shells

These fragile, wedge-shaped shells live in soft sandy mud in warm, deep water. Although rare on the Pacific Coast, these three species are commonly found in the Atlantic. Pens attach themselves to buried rocks or stones with a byssus made of olive-golden threads that grow out of the small end of their shell. In ancient Rome, these threads were woven into golden-colored caps and gloves; byssal threads may even have made up the mythological golden fleece sought by Jason. Pen snails have a large muscle which, like the muscle in a scallop, is good to eat. They have been known to produce black pearls.

Saw-toothed Pen Shell
Color the outside of this pen shell yellow-brown to gray-brown. Shell 6 to 12 in. long; found from North Carolina to Texas, and in South America. (198)

Stiff Pen Shell
A dark olive-brown shell, 5 to 11 in. long. Found from North Carolina to the Caribbean. (199)

Amber Pen Shell
Color this shell pale pinkish orange to amber. Shell 4 to 11 in. long; found from southeastern Florida to the Caribbean. (200)

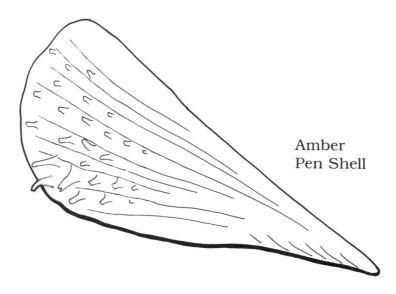

Amber
Pen Shell

Thorny Oyster Shells

A small family of mollusks, related to scallops. These oysters have a series of light-sensitive eyes along the outer edge of the shell's inner lining. The shells have a ball-and-socket hinge. Thorny oysters attach themselves to rocks, coral, or other shells in shallow to very deep water, in warm seas. In calm waters, they develop long, brightly colored spines, which inspired their other name: chrysanthemum shells.

Pacific Thorny Oyster

The spines on this shell are less than 1½ in. long. Color it brownish rose to orangish rose. Shell 1½ to 5½ in. long; found in deep water from Baja California to Panama. (201)

Atlantic Thorny Oyster

This shell's spines grow up to 3 in. long. The outside is white, with yellow and yellow-orange spines. Shell 1½ to 5½ in. long; found from North Carolina to the Caribbean. (202)

Pacific
Thorny Oyster

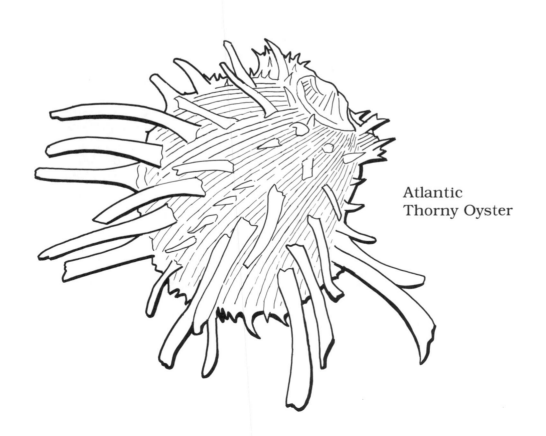

Atlantic
Thorny Oyster

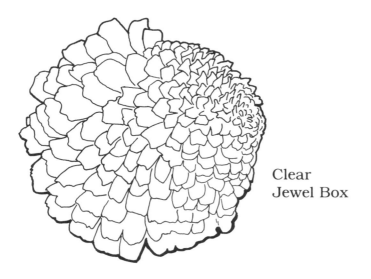

Clear
Jewel Box

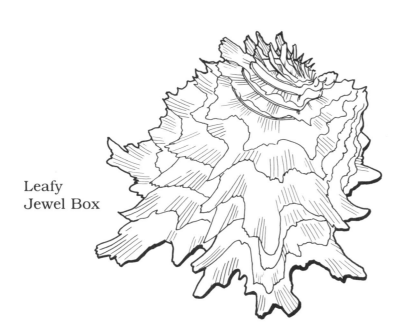

Leafy
Jewel Box

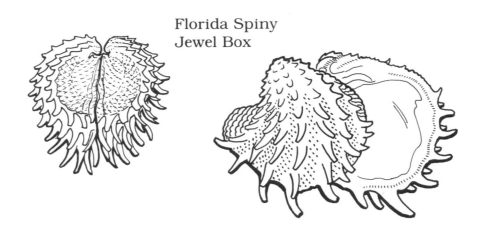

Florida Spiny
Jewel Box

Jewel Box Shells

These bivalves cement them-selves to rocks, coral, other shells, sturdy plants, ship-wrecks, or any hard surface. A hammer and chisel are needed to separate them. Their thick, heavy shells are white or pastel-colored, with two valves of different sizes — the anchoring shell is the larger and deeper of the two. All jewel box shells are frilly, leafy, or spiny, and they may have circular rows of flattened, platelike, or bladelike spines. In some species, the inside of the shell resembles translucent white china. These shells are found in shallow to deep water, in tropical and temper-ate areas.

Clear Jewel Box
A translucent white shell, tinged with pink and pinkish yellow to deep peach. Shell 1½ to 3½ in. long; found from Ore-gon to Baja California. (203)

Leafy Jewel Box
The color of this shell varies from white to yellow, orange, rose, or pink. It may also be all dusty rose. Shell 1¼ to 3½ in. long; found from the Florida coastline to Brazil. (204)

Florida Spiny Jewel Box
The outside of this jewel box shell is white. Inside, it is white with a purple and wine-colored stain. Shell 1 to 2½ in. long; found from North Carolina to Mexico. (205)

Jingle Shells

Very thin, irregularly shaped, sugary-looking shells, with a bright pearly luster. A hole in the lower shell shows where a large, stubby byssus anchored the animal in life. Unlike mussels, jingle snails cannot break their byssus and are permanently fixed in place.

Common Jingle
This jingle shell varies from silvery white or yellow to orange. Shell ¾ to 2¼ in. long; found from Massachusetts to Brazil. (206)

Kitten Paw Shells

A small family of thick, fan-shaped shells with strong ribs. The mollusk cements its shell to a rock or any hard surface.

Kitten's Paw
Color this shell creamy tan, with fine reddish brown lines. Shell ¾ to 1½ in. high; found from North Carolina to the West Indies. (207)

Wing Oyster Shells

Thick shells, thin on the edges. All species have a strong byssal-thread anchor, an outer skin, and precious mother-of-pearl on the inside of the shell. These inedible oysters live in tropical waters.

Atlantic Wing Oyster
The color of this shell varies from pale yellow or brown to purple-brown. Shell 1½ to 3½ in. long; found from North Carolina to Brazil. (208)

Western Wing Oyster
Color this oyster shell deep purplish brown, with paler rays. Shell 3 to 4 in. long; found from California to Canada. (209)

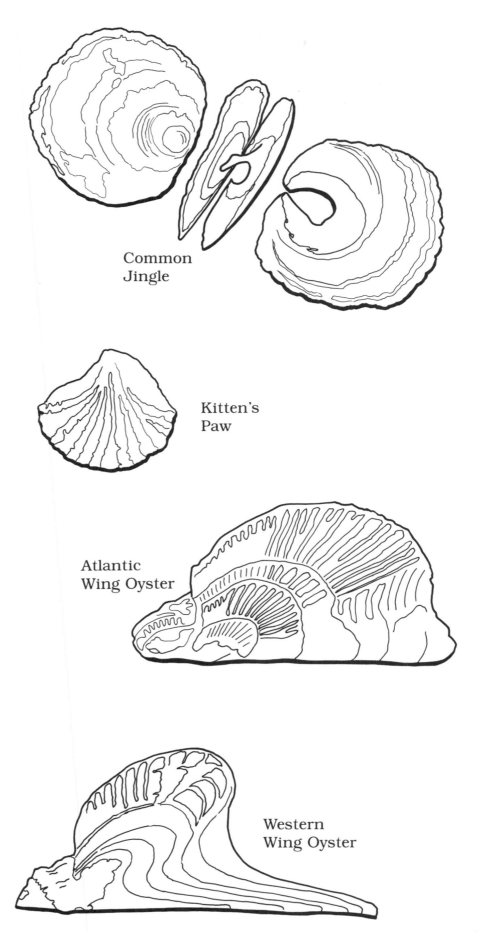

Common Jingle

Kitten's Paw

Atlantic Wing Oyster

Western Wing Oyster

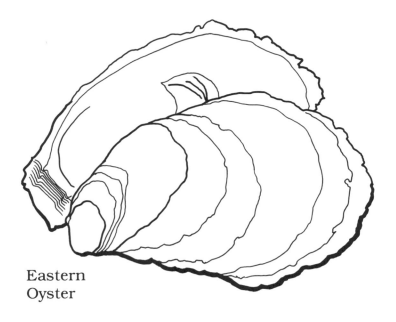

Eastern
Oyster

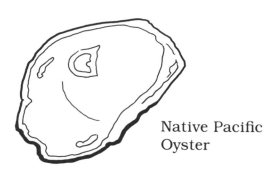

Native Pacific
Oyster

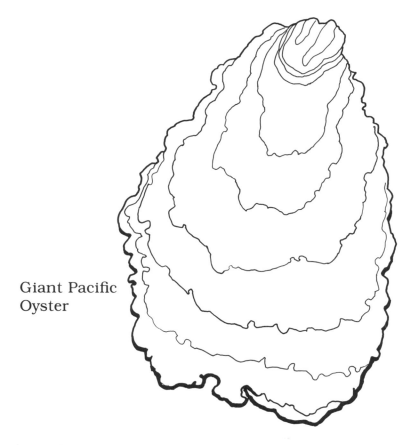

Giant Pacific
Oyster

Oyster Shells

Oysters are a delicious source of food and the most valuable bivalves in the seafood industry. Harvested by tongs, dredges, or skin divers, they are found in the shallow warmer waters of all oceans, except in the Arctic and Antarctic.

Oysters are both male and female at different times in their life span. The young swim freely until they attach themselves to something solid — such as another shell, a rock, or a root — for the rest of their lives. Oysters are eaten by many creatures, including starfish, clams, other shellfish, crabs, worms, fish, sponges, birds, and man. They may also be harmed by water that is too salty or not salty enough, and by disease.

Each oyster shell varies in shape because of living conditions and growth patterns. The lower shell is deeper than the upper, which is sometimes slightly flat.

Eastern Oyster
The outside of this shell is white to greenish brown or dirty gray. Inside, it is white with a purple muscle scar and edging. Shell 2 to 8 in. long; found from Canada to the Gulf of Mexico. (210)

Native Pacific Oyster
The inside is stained with different shades of olive green, with a tinge of rainbow-like iridescence. Shell 1½ to 3½ in. long; found from Alaska to Baja California. (211)

Giant Pacific Oyster
This shell is also called the Japanese Oyster. Color it dirty white to brownish gray. Shell 3 to 12 in. long; found from Canada to California. (212)

Tusk Shells

Tusk shells are delicate, slightly curved, and open at both ends. Also called "tooth shells," they may be smooth, ribbed, glossy or dull, but are usually white. Some tropical varieties are tinged with color.

These mollusks live partially buried under sand with the small end of the shell up. They circulate water through a hole in this small end. A wormlike foot protrudes from the large end of the shell, and is used for burrowing.

Indians of the Pacific Northwest used tusk shells for money, and cut them into sections to make beads for jewelry. These shells are found worldwide in seas, in shallow to deep water.

Indian Money Tusk
A white shell, 1 to 2½ in. long. Found from Alaska to Mexico. (213)

Florida Tusk
This tusk shell is yellowish white. A rare shell, 2 to 3 in. long; found from Florida to the Caribbean. (214)

Texas Tusk
Color this shell grayish white. Shell ¾ to 1½ in. long; found from North Carolina to the Gulf States. (215)

Ivory Tusk
This shell is ivory white to pinkish. Shell 1 to 2 in. long; found from North Carolina to southwestern Florida and south to the West Indies. (216)

Shining Tusk
A perfectly smooth, creamy white shell. Shell 2 in. long; found in the Gulf of Mexico. (217)

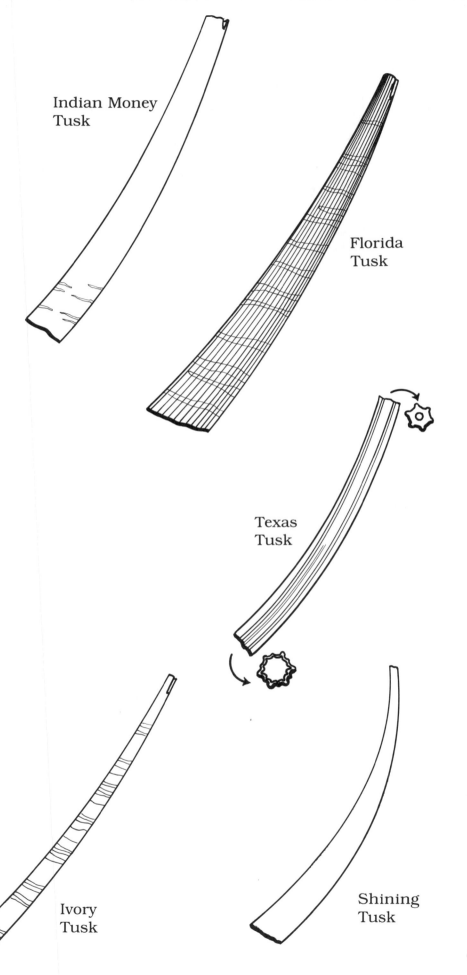

Indian Money Tusk

Florida Tusk

Texas Tusk

Ivory Tusk

Shining Tusk

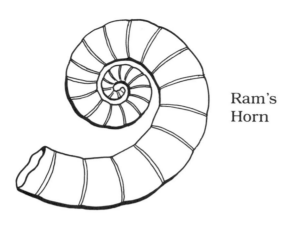

Ram's
Horn

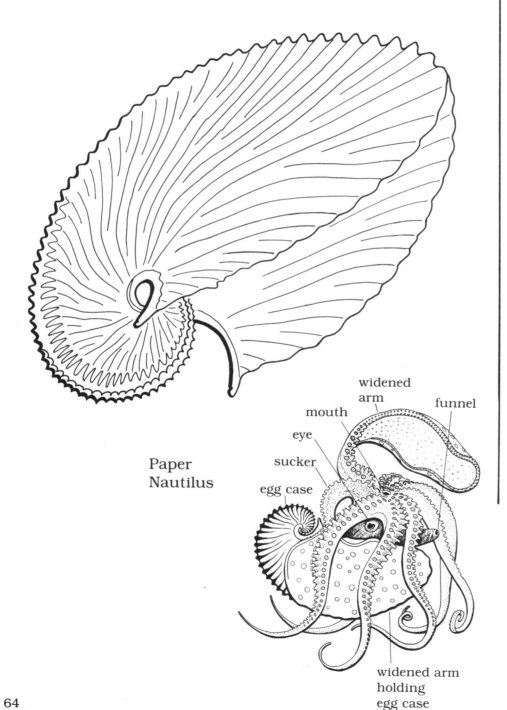

Paper
Nautilus

widened
arm

funnel

mouth

eye

sucker

egg case

widened arm
holding
egg case

Cephalopods

The class Cephalopoda contains the most highly developed of the mollusks, including the Octopus, Squid, and Cuttlefish. All have eight or more arms surrounding their mouth. Most cephalopods have no outside shell, but grow a thin, platelike shell called the "pen" inside their body.

Cephalopods are found worldwide in warm and temperate seas. Several kinds of squid and these two shell-bearing species are found on our shores.

Spirula Ram's Horn

This small, chambered, white shell called a Ram's Horn is embedded in the rear part of the Spirula's body. It may be used for balance. Shell 1 in. in diameter; found from Cape Cod to Florida. (218)

Paper Nautilus

This animal is also called the Paper Argonaut. Neither the male nor the female has a true outer shell, but the female secretes a sticky white substance out of two of her eight arms which hardens into a thin, shell-like egg case. She cradles this shelly "nest" in these two webbed, widened arms, and the young develop there until they can care for themselves. The female then releases the empty case and it floats away. Color the egg case milky white tinged with brown. Shell (egg case) up to 8 in. in diameter; it washes up on shores and beaches from Florida to New Jersey. (219)